Joseph Hatton

Cigarette papers for after-dinner smoking

Second Edition

Joseph Hatton

Cigarette papers for after-dinner smoking
Second Edition

ISBN/EAN: 9783337132293

Printed in Europe, USA, Canada, Australia, Japan

Cover: Foto ©Andreas Hilbeck / pixelio.de

More available books at **www.hansebooks.com**

A QUIET PIPE. [*See p.* 255.

CIGARETTE PAPERS

FOR AFTER-DINNER SMOKING.

BY

JOSEPH HATTON,

AUTHOR OF
"BY ORDER OF THE CZAR," "CLYTIE," "OLD LAMPS AND NEW,"
"TOOLE'S REMINISCENCES," ETC.

WITH EIGHTY ILLUSTRATIONS

BY E. RAVEN HILL, A. J. FINBERG, J. L. SCLANDERS,
AND JOHN WALLACE.

SECOND EDITION.

LONDON:
HUTCHINSON & CO.,
25, PATERNOSTER SQUARE.
1892.

"For Auld Lang Syne,"

THESE FUGITIVE SKETCHES ARE

DEDICATED TO

TOM D. TAYLOR,

IN TOKEN OF THE AUTHOR'S

PERSONAL REGARD.

PROHIBITED IN RUSSIA.

Thirteenth Edition. Cloth gilt, 2s. 6d., paper boards, 2s.

BY ORDER OF THE CZAR.

The Tragic Story of Anna Klosstock, Queen of the Ghetto.

By JOSEPH HATTON.

Mr. L. J. Jennings, M.P., in the *New York Herald*, says:—"The entire story has been worked out with the greatest care, and its development shows not only practised literary skill, but great knowledge of the world. It may, in some degree, do for Russian despotism what 'Uncle Tom's Cabin' did for slavery."

Mr. Gladstone writes:—"That he hopes the book may have a good influence on the policy of Russia towards the Jews."

SECOND EDITION.

Crown 8vo, cloth gilt extra, 6s.

OLD LAMPS AND NEW:

Notes and Reminiscences.

By JOSEPH HATTON.

WITH PORTRAIT OF THE AUTHOR.

"As entertaining a light volume as we have often read."—*Times.*

"Among recent volumes of a reminiscent cast, 'Old Lamps and New' is the freshest and pleasantest."—*Saturday Review.*

"There are reminiscences of a holiday spent with Henry Irving, of Victor Hugo, and of Sothern; 'At Home' sketches of William Black, Miss Braddon, and Tennyson; the story of Mr. Labouchere's life—and a funny story it is; a criticism of Ouida, and some early life and other recollections of the author. Mr. Hatton very soon gets on happy terms with his readers; he writes in an easy, chatty style; and over these sketches one may while away a very pleasant hour."—*Pall Mall Gazette.*

LONDON: HUTCHINSON & CO., 25, PATERNOSTER SQUARE.

CONTENTS.

I.

INTRODUCTORY.

                                                                                      PAGE

An Invitation—Fact and Fancy—Silent Companionship—Harmless Narcotics—Not yet " Prohibited in Russia "—The *Novoe Vremya*—My friend Fox 1

II.

SOME THEATRICAL REMINISCENCES.

Webster and Mark Lemon—A Psychological Study—*The Dead Heart*—Toole and Paul Bedford—A Story of the Green-Room—Truth Stranger than Fiction—The Vengeance of a Quiet Man—Webster's Latest Banquet—" To His Majesty the King ! " 6

III.

A FAMOUS RECORD.

George Augustus Sala—A Hard Fight and a Glorious Victory—The Beginning of a Literary Career—It was "The Key of the Street " that opened the door—Charles Dickens and the first Five-pound Note Sala ever earned—Sala tells his own Story—Literary Journalism 19

IV.

AMERICANS IN LONDON.

First Experiences—" I shall have some funny things to tell them home " —Policemen, Cabs, and the Irish Question—" So

Solid "—Winter's " Trip to England "—A Tribute to the Old
Country—Reminiscences of Home the Spiritualist . . 28

V.

LITERARY MEN AND ACTORS.

Fox is of Opinion that Literary Men and Actors should not
Marry — Actresses' Husbands — The old Fashion—Lady
Beaconsfield, Mrs. Gladstone, and other Famous Wives—
Shrews and Helpmates 40

VI.

THE BATTLE OF LONDON.

The Story of Sir Augustus Harris - A Business Man—Earnestness
and Energy—Audacity Difficulty—The Fight—A Walk in
the Park—Ups and Downs—Success—Stage-work, Past,
Present, and French 48

VII.

"THE STAR OF SOUTH AFRICA."

A word with the *Cornhill*—The Koh-i-noor and the "Porter
Rhodes "—Off-colour—The Beginning of Diamond Mining
at the Cape—" O'Reilly's Folly "—Fever—A Note of Comfort—And otherwise 67

VIII.

CHARLES READE, AND " NABOTH'S VINEYARD."

Reade's Favourite Home—" A Dramatist by Natural Gift a
Novelist by Force of Circumstances "—The Private Bill
Demon—" Readiana "—From Albert Gate to Knightsbridge
—" And I got Five Pounds for it "—Gardening and Literature—Wilkie Collins at Home—" Walker " 78

IX.

" AS YOU LIKE IT " AT POPE'S VILLA.

A Reminiscence of the Thames—Mrs. Langtry and Outdoor Plays
—Under the Elms—A Lesson in Shakespeare—The First

Rehearsal—Mrs. Labouchere and her Pupil—Personal Beauty
—Can Acting be Taught? 90

X.

"BETWEEN THE ACTS."

My Friend Fox is Critical—Women's Friendships—At Marlborough House—"Good morning!" Not Worth the Candle
—Mrs. Tufthunter-Bragg—The Marriage Market—"Forgive
the Preacher for the sake of Fox". 100

XI.

A CHAT WITH A PUBLISHER.

The Story of a Book—Ouida "First"—In a Popular Publisher's
Room—From a Window in Piccadilly—Ouida and the Proprieties—"Little Wooden Shoes" and "A Dog of Flanders" 107

XII.

CRITICS CRITICISED.

The Publisher and the Press—Library Readers of Fiction—The
Potentiality of the Novel—Author and Publisher—An
Honest Sentiment 116

XIII.

THE SALVATION ARMY.

A Remarkable Organisation — Fanatic or Philanthropist?—
Revivalism—Dinah Morris and Circe—Refuges for the
Lost 124

XIV.

HOW IT ORIGINATED.

Mr. Booth and His Recruits—The Army—The General Regulations—"Chuckers Out"—Suggestions—What Fox Thinks
about it—"In Darkest England" 132

XV.

THE GOOD OLD DAYS.

A Novel Exhibition—The Norwich Coach and the Cheltenham Rival—" The Fly "—The first Mail Coaches—" Fox says the Coach is a Fraud nevertheless " 143

XVI.

MANY THOUGHTS ON MANY THINGS.

Don't be Successful—The Unappreciated—An Age of Gossip—Fox Intervenes—The Novel of the Future—A New Literary Era—Bateman and *Charles the First*—A Reminiscence of Cyfarthfa—At Supper with Irving—" To meet the Count, Countess, and Baron Magri "—The Trees at Bournemouth . 153

XVII.

"LET US TAKE A WALK DOWN FLEET STREET."

Richardson's Printing Office—Where Dr. Johnson first met Boswell—Famous Names—In the Footsteps of Dickens—Hepworth Dixon and " Ruby Grey "—In the Temple—Law and Revel 177

XVIII.

FROM THE GRIFFIN TO COVENT GARDEN.

Glimpses of the Strand—Where Dr. Johnson Worshipped—Editors of *Punch*—Jumbo and Chunee—Past and Present—Historic Streets—Mrs. Lirriper and Sir Roger de Coverley . 193

XIX.

IN THE DEPARTMENT OF CALVADOS.

From London to Caen—A Feast of Lanterns—Pictures at Midnight and After—*La Voiture de M. Cabieux*—The Onion Fair—Cities and their Physiognomy—The Splendid Confusion—" Challenged at the Grave "—A Terrible Story . 206

XX.
STRANGE DREAMS.

"The Children of an Idle Brain"—In the Regions of Absurdity—Prophetic of Death—A Reminiscence of the Caskets—Tragedy—Strange Coincidences—What are Dreams? Problems Solved in Sleep 230

XXI.
COMING INTO MONEY.

The Slot of Fortune—Fox's One Bet—The Poor Man and his £20,000—What it feels like to come into a Fortune—Sydney Smith and his Yorkshire Living—Coming Events . 243

XXII.
"A QUIET PIPE."

Spurgeon and Carlyle on Tobacco—"Smoke and Poesy"—"A Cigarette-maker's Romance"—"Cope's Smoke-room Booklets"—A Whistlerian Inspiration—A Flower from "The Smoker's Garland"—James Thompson, the Poet—Tarass Bulba Schmidt 255

XXIII.
"SHE WAS A BEAUTIFUL WOMAN."

Fox and an Interesting Prisoner—Snobs and "Local Lords"—"The Wild West"—A Lady of Birth and Wealth—A Photograph—She calls!—Wants to be an Actress and start a Paper—She tells her Story—I introduce her to a Great Lawyer—Suspected, Denounced: Prosperous and Scornful nevertheless—During the Merry Days of a Prosperous Season Fox speaks again 270

XXIV.
LOST IN LONDON.

Burlesque and Art—Leslie and the Master—A Subject for a Novel—Drama in Real Life—An Incident of Victoria Station—Men and Women who Disappear—"Save me!" . . 285

XXV.

FOUND IN GERMANY.

PAGE

Fox continues his Exciting Story—Worse than Death—A New Anaesthetic—Mother and Father—A Strange Feature of the Case—The Fiend who spoke French with a Foreign Accent   293

XXVI.

THE END OF THE DRAMA.

Cui Bono? Questions of the Day and the Story of Victoria Station—Fox and Monsieur X———They discuss the French and English Systems, and Fox makes a Discovery—The Wretch meets his Master—Truth and Fiction—Finis   .   300

"CIGARETTE PAPERS."

I.

INTRODUCTORY.

An Invitation—Fact and Fancy—Silent Companionship.—Harmless Narcotics—Not yet "Prohibited in Russia."—The *Novoe Vremya*—My friend Fox.

I.

'T is not necessary that you should be a smoker to extract from these papers whatever they may contain of postprandial trifling or literary enjoyment. There is much virtue in tobacco, but there are wise men and lovely women who have never rolled a cigarette, nor dreamed an hour away behind a mild cigar. They have found their sedatives in other things: in sermons, perhaps, or in some choice and dainty *liqueur.* If, however, you should be accustomed to seek the solace of the golden weed, and let your fancy tinge " the wreathed smoke " with calm reflective thought, then mayhap you shall find in these "Cigarette Papers" a passing fact or fancy, a wayside reminiscence, an anecdote, an epigram, a story, or a scrap of what is called philosophy. If the resultant be to your liking, I beg you will roll it up with your cigarette, or drop it into your pipe and smoke it.

II.

What journeys they have made, some of these "Cigarette Papers"! I have envied them "many a time and oft." They have started on adventurous voyages, and while fulfilling their mission have been detained by friends or captured by pirates, to enter upon fresh careers. Knowing their soothing qualities—antidotes to insomnia, mild encouragers of sleep, harmless narcotics—it has cheered me to have tidings of them from miners' huts in the Rocky Mountains, from beneath the awnings of lazy canoes in Eastern seas, silent companions of weary travellers; useful adjuncts to—

> " Sublime tobacco, which from East to West
> Cheers the tar's labour or the Turkman's rest."

Not as a matter of pride, but as a piece of interesting information, I deem it right to give you what may be called the pedigree of these notes which you are invited

to smoke with your varied weeds. You like to know
the record of a horse, the pedigree of a dog. The brand
on a cigar box is to all of us an important guarantee
of its contents. Similarly, I would have you know
where these printed trifles have originated, and what
famous houses have given them their imprimatur.
If I sometimes wonder whether they were worth so
wide a distribution as they have obtained, I never
doubt their somnolent qualities, in which I find my
best excuse for offering a parcel of them bound
together for convenient use.

III.

Not a few of these texts for chat—papers for the
burning—are fresh and up to date; others first saw
the light in the *New York Times*. One or two have
appeared in the *New York Herald*; several owe their
origin to journals in Chicago, Washington, and Phila-
delphia. Many were prepared for the cigarette cases
of *Umpire* readers, and, in company with a story by
Bret Harte, did duty for some pages of *Pick-Me-Up*,
which adorned them with pictorial illustration. Here
and there, personal notes which I contributed during
several years of London correspondentship for the
Sydney Morning Herald of New South Wales, and
the *Kreuz Zeitung* of Berlin, are introduced. The
balance, I think, have had endorsement in *Harper's*,
the *Argosy*, the *Theatre*, and other popular magazines;

but for this handy volume they are retrimmed, recut, and made suitable for an extended patronage of new smokers, and for renewed introduction to those who are already acquainted with their claims to public approval—or otherwise.

"Prohibited in Russia" still marks the pages of "By Order of the Czar"; but the publishers of these present pages need not fear that the Imperial Censor will find reason to put a ban upon this collected bundle of Cigarette Papers, the quality of which has already been tested and approved by the *Novoe Vremya*, which would be a fine, enterprising, newsy, and influential European journal if the Censorship would give it a chance. I have always thought there was something more than compliment to the author and his work in the *Novoe Vremya's* republication of several chapters of "Journalistic London," which contained a lesson of newspaper liberty that Russians may yet live to see fruitful in the vast territories of the Czar.

IV.

After-dinner chat, in the opinion of my friend, Mr. William Fox, should be retrospective in spirit and prophetic in character. It should continually cast the shadow of the past over the future. I have great respect for the opinion of Mr. Fox. He is learned from an academic point of view, and he knows the world. How much he knows of books and men, of women and fashions, of society, and the city, you will learn in course of time. He is a man among men —clever, discreet, learned, a diplomat, and he likes me. There is no secret, personal or otherwise, which he fears to entrust to my keeping. There is not one item of his confidential communications that he knows I will not use if possible; but he winks at my infidelities, so long as I disguise names and localities, and use his experiences for the amusement of the public. He is a capital fellow, Fox; you must have met him in a quiet way in "The Gay World." A short, dapper little man, you know, foxy somewhat in appearance, having a curious habit of accentuating the points of his remarks with a snappish closing of his mouth that reminded you of a fox-terrier with a bad temper and sharp teeth; a good fellow for all that, and I want you to like him; he knows so much! We must be friends, all of us. He will introduce us, perhaps, to Loftus Kennett, Joe Drayton, Harvey Pepys, Eric Yorke, and no end of clever and entertaining men. But whether he enlarges the circle of our personal acquaintance or not, he is a host in himself, as you shall find.

II.

SOME THEATRICAL REMINISCENCES.

Webster and Mark Lemon—A Psychological Study—*The Dead Heart*—Toole and Paul Bedford—A Story of the Green-Room—Truth Stranger than Fiction—The Vengeance of a Quiet Man—Webster's Latest Banquet—"To His Majesty the King!"

I.

Touching the influence of the past on the after-dinner chat of the present, a recent revival of *The Dead Heart* set me thinking in that direction of retrospect and reminiscence which seems to have a special charm for the modern reader. I enjoyed the intimate friendship of Benjamin Webster, have frequently stood at the Adelphi prompt wing and seen him act. He was an old friend of Mark Lemon in my earliest London days. Mark had a key to his private door in Maiden Lane, and that was our way into the Adelphi. I did not see Webster's original production of *The Dead Heart*, but I was present on the first night of the revival, when Arthur Stirling played the part of the Abbé de Latour, which Mr. Irving entrusted to the artistic interpretation of Mr.

Bancroft, whose return to the stage for that performance was a notable incident of a very interesting season. Mrs. Alfred Mellon was the Countess de St. Valerie, and John Billington was her son. In the Lyceum revival Miss Ellen Terry played Mrs. Mellon's part, and her son the young Count, which gave great actuality to the scenes in which they appeared. Miss Terry's supreme charm as an actress, apart from her intellectuality and artistic appreciation, is her womanliness, her sympathetic realisation of a pathetic incident.

Of late one has heard much about psychological studies on the stage. I mentioned the other week in the *Sunday Times* that I remember the use of the term for the first time in dramatic criticism in John Oxenford's *Times* notice of *The Dead Heart*, and he applied it especially to Webster's acting in the scene after the taking of the Bastille, when Robert Landry (the hero of the story), a grey-bearded broken man, is brought forth from a living grave. He had been incarcerated, through the instrumentality of the villain of the story, on the eve of a marriage of love. "A word from a king's mistress, a scratch from a king's pen," and Robert, a young artist, full of vigour, with brilliant possibilities in a rosy future, was snatched away and plunged into a living tomb. The world, busy with its million occupations, soon forgot the poor sculptor. Men strove and thrived, or strove and failed, sought the sweet companionship of women, married, and gazed on the faces of their children. Life rolled on, ever changing but for him. He alone sat in the darkness—a cannibal devouring his own heart. At last the people plucked him from the tomb; but his heart was dead. It was in his return to the light of heaven that Webster realised Oxenford's idea of a psychological study; and there is no doubt the scene was one of the most legitimate of histrionic triumphs. Mr. Irving has the very qualities that enabled Webster to achieve it. He has great moments, a singular power of suggesting introspection, a natural love of what is weird, and a keen artistic sense of what is both tragic and pathetic.

II.

There is nothing more touching in the entire range of melodrama than the two scenes in the last act. Robert Landry is in power. The son of the woman he loved, and from whom he was snatched away by the man who married her, is in the Conciergerie awaiting death. Robert Landry, in his office, rises now and then to go to the window and look out. The night is far advanced. It is moonlight. Outside the prison a woman is seated, solitary and alone, upon the steps by the prison gate, a pathetic picture of misery. It is the Countess, waiting to say farewell to her son, when the tumbril shall come to carry him to the guillotine. Landry looks out and sees the poor creature. "That woman there still! Still seated upon the same stone. Some unfortunate, the whole of whose little world is contained within these sombre walls. She has not changed her position since I observed her an hour ago. Ah! the weary, weary watching when love sits sorrowing at the prison gate. She turns her face this way; perhaps the light attracts her, poor woman! No beacon of hope can shine from such a place as this." But presently his heart is stirred with new life, it beats to new and glorious sensations; and when the curtain falls it is he, instead of the widow's son, who stands upon the scaffold, a martyr to love and boyish dreams. Mr. Dickens got his inspiration for the most dramatic and stirring of all his works, "A Tale of Two Cities," from Watts Phillips's *Dead Heart*; and Clayton's famous last scene in *All for Her* was an artistic reminiscence of Benjamin Webster in the last act of the Adelphi drama. From the corridor of the prison the back of the stage opens, and discovers a view of the guillotine, guarded by gendarmes and sectionaries, and surrounded by the mob. The tall, quaint old houses of the great city are just touched by the first rays of early morning, which cover the tower of Notre Dame with a crimson glow. In the background, upon the scaffold, stands Robert Landry, prepared for the fatal axe. He extends his arms in the direction

of the weeping Countess as the curtain falls. All
this, however, would be as nothing if it were not the
dénouement of a strong dramatic story.

III.

It is of *The Dead Heart* that Toole tells a theatrical

BETWEEN THE ACTS.

story, which is a painful illustration, in its way, of the
short step from the sublime to the ridiculous. "It
was at the time when one of those catch sayings or
street gags was in vogue, 'How's your poor feet?'—an
idiotic question which *gamins* put to each other
without rhyme or reason. 'My heart is dead,' said
Webster, in the play, and with his usual thrilling

emphasis. In the midst of the solemn silence a gallery boy called out, 'How's your poor feet?' Webster growled anathemas not loud but deep, and the audience let the remark pass without either a laugh or a hush. In the excitement of the scene probably but few of them heard it. We were all on the stage, Paul Bedford and myself among the rest— it was the revolutionary scene—the piece had had a long run, we had nothing to do in the scene, and we could not restrain our laughter; but I need not say we did not indulge our mirth in sight of the audience, nor did we mean Webster to see it, but he did, and went to his room including us in his growls at 'idiots who would laugh at a funeral, or grin at a murder, heartless fools!' Soon afterwards, however, he smiled at the incident himself."

IV.

When I think of Webster it always occurs to me to reflect upon the might-have-beens in life, and to wonder if we had not taken this or that turning on the great highway what would have happened, what difference there would have been in our positions, and where we should have landed. Webster told me that, when a boy, he saw Rolla performed at Birmingham, and there and then made up his mind to be an actor, more particularly for the purpose of playing Rolla. He ran away from home, bought a sword for the part of Rolla, and walking to his first engagement, in a wooden house at Bromsgrove or Kidderminster, or somewhere in that neighbourhood, had to sell his kit, everything, to pay his way; everything but the sword which he intended to use in the part of Rolla. In due course he became a popular actor and manager in London; but he never played Rolla.

"In the days of Webster's impecuniosity," said Mark Lemon one day during a chat at the Tavistock, "Ben used to enjoy for dinner the part of an ox called, I think, the milt. I often mentioned to my wife Ben's praises of this cheap and savoury dish." Turning then to me, he said, "You once wrote some articles on cheap dishes; well, you should try the dish Webster almost lived on in his strolling days." Webster laughed, and then pulled a wry face. "I induced my wife to get this choice piece of food and cook it one day when Ben came to dine with us. Ben rubbed his hands with delight when it was placed upon the table; we all tasted it; the result was, to use a vulgar phrase, simply beastly!"

"It was all a question of appetite, I suppose," said Webster; "how they devour those 'pennorths o' puddin'' and those 'savoury meat pies' in the Eastend!"

"All," as Webster said, "a question of appetite"—"and custom" one might add, having regard to certain revelations from the Congo.

V.

Webster was a great actor. He often wept copiously in pathetic scenes, and he was tremendously in earnest in all his business. When Arthur Stirling played the Abbé in *The Dead Heart*, Webster, who was an expert swordsman, always ran Stirling through in a

A TRAGEDY.

certain part of his garment, right under the arm; only those who knew Arthur and Webster would probably notice the little tremor of nervousness with which Stirling received his death blow. In the days when Webster dominated the hearts and souls of Adelphi audiences, now in *The Willow Copse*, now in

Janet Pride, now in *The Dead Heart*, he used to tell a dramatic story that I often promised him and myself I would write in full, and which I am going to print in this place at the risk of being charged with repeating myself, and introducing some of my readers to what the Americans call a chestnut.

Webster always believed some one had written it and spoiled it, but I have never come across the narrative, nor met any one who has. I have learnt recently that Charles Dickens would occasionally narrate it as one of Webster's stories, and always with an intense relish. It floats in my mind somewhat vaguely in the following shape:—

A certain young fellow named Johnson, a man-about-town, of independent fortune, had the *entrée* of the green-room. He was looked upon as a harmless, pleasant gentleman, and he was popular with the leading artistes of the theatre.

One evening a member of the company read from a newspaper an account of a notable and tragic duel in France. The combatants were a practised French duellist and a young Englishman.

On the ground the Frenchman had walked up to his opponent, who was little more than a youth, laid his hand on his heart, and said, "Ah! you are courageous, I see. Have you a mother?"

"Yes! I am her only son," was the reply.

"Ah!" said the duellist, "I am sorry; I shall hit

you just there by the third button of your coat. In five minutes from now your mother will be childless!"

It was a cruelly true forecast. The English boy was killed.

Mr. Johnson, leaning against the green room mantel-

THE AVENGER.

shelf, looked up when the reader had finished the recital.

"Ah!" he said, "the brute! I will kill him."

I do not profess to repeat the story as Webster told it to me, but to give the spirit of it. The next night Mr. Johnson did not appear in the green-room, nor on the next night, nor for many nights.

"Where is Johnson?" asked everybody.

Inquiries were made at his rooms. Nobody knew where Johnson was. By-and-bye he reappeared in his favourite attitude, leaning against the fireplace.

"Ah, back again!" exclaimed the artistes. "Where have you been?"

"To France," said Mr. Johnson.

"To France! what for?"

They had forgotten the dead boy of the duel.

"To kill that fellow!" he said.

It was true. He went to Paris the very night he heard the newspaper paragraph read, found out his man, insulted him, was called out to the same field where his young countryman had fallen. Prior to the fight he had gone up to the Frenchman, laid his hand on his heart, asked if he had a mother, and indicated the button beneath which he would strike him. The Frenchman fell dead at Johnson's first shot. Whereupon the Englishman had returned to his pleasant corner by the mantelpiece of the green-room fire.

VI.

My friend Fox thinks this is one of my best stories. I make no claim to it. The facts are true. Perhaps it is well that they should be thus briefly narrated. Fox says he felt uncomfortable when he saw how prominently I had introduced him to the public. But he likes me too well to dispute my judgment, and he thinks it possible that he may after all be able to provide me with a few notes for the new work. He says he dined at the Langham with Mr. Richard Mansfield, on the last night of *Richard III.* at the Globe, and that he spent a singularly interesting evening. Max O'Rell was there. A shrewd, thoughtful man, Max O'Rell; but he thinks we are spoiling him when we permit him to denounce the Derby crowd as he has done in the *Pall Mall.* A capital paper the *P.M.G.*, up to every journalistic device to make its pages interesting and useful. According to Max O'Rell, the Epsom crowd was a brutal, fighting, dirty mob, kind to its horses, but only because it was itself animal. This is a trifle strong, but Max does not mean to go to the Derby any more, so he will escape the attentions of the crowd. Otherwise Fox says he would not like to be responsible for his safety next year. Did I ever see a welsher in active trouble? At the supper in question Max O'Rell was smart, bright, clever, said risky things "with a snap," as the Yankees have it; and was just as successful as Toole, who told the company the difference between the sensations of a low comedian when business is bad, and how a tragedian feels about it. Mansfield was very happy in his after-supper oratory, as also were Joseph Knight and Beerbohm Tree; not to mention Gilbert the sculptor, and Mr. Dam, of the *New York Times*, a capable journalist, who intends to found, for the benefit of the craft, a supper club, at which Mr.

Fox hopes to be a constant attendant. Fox, by the way, says I ought not to omit one of the most pathetic and characteristic stories of the last days of Webster. Shortly before his death he presided at the annual dinner of the "Drury Lane Fund" at Richmond, and when he rose to propose the first loyal toast of the

BENJAMIN WEBSTER.

evening he was a little rambling in his speech, seemed to be looking far away with his great eloquent eyes, and when he sat down he said, "Gentlemen, I will now call upon you to drink to the health of his Majesty *The King!*" His thoughts had gone back to those early days we were talking about just now; he was for the moment young again, and our gracious Queen was still a school-girl at Bath.

III.

A FAMOUS RECORD.

George Augustus Sala — A Hard Fight and a Glorious Victory — The Beginning of a Literary Career — It was "The Key of the Street" that opened the door — Charles Dickens and the first Five-pound Note Sala ever earned — Sala tells his own Story — Literary Journalism.

I.

IF your story is to be told it is perhaps better to tell it yourself than to leave it to be narrated by some one else when you are no longer alive to revise the proofs. Whether it is the warning example of "Froude on Carlyle" that has set everybody off relating their own histories, or whether there is a rush of "reminiscencers" who think nobody would be likely to put them into a book if they did not do it

GEORGE AUGUSTUS SALA.

themselves, it is not for me to conjecture. Nothing is more interesting than personal records of the battle of life when there has been a battle worth fighting, and well fought. Next to that kind of book is a journal of the man who has lived behind the scenes of politics, literature, and art, who has travelled, and who has something new to say about the work he has done and the remarkable people he has met; and such a book should be the reminiscences of Mr. G. A. Sala. The well-known journalist and author had in his early days a hard fight, and won a glorious victory; but the people he has known, the things he has seen, the incidents in which he has had a part, are connected with the history of our times— all these matters overshadow in interest the mere records of how he won his literary spurs. Mr. Frith, Mr. and Mrs. Bancroft, Mr. John Coleman, and Mr. Yates, have recently given us their stories of art and actors. Mr. Sala's varied history of men and things has yet to come. It will not be out of place to suggest to the general reader the *raison d'être* of Mr. Sala's "Life and Times."

II.

A cheery, middle-aged man, with a busy manner, Mr. George Augustus Sala is one of the most familiar figures in the artistic, literary, and general society of the metropolis. He has had a very exceptional career, but is best known as a leader-writer and special correspondent on the staff of the *Daily Telegraph*. Educated abroad, he began his artistic labours at a very early age. While quite a boy he was engaged as a caricaturist by a leading publisher. At a later date he became assistant scene-painter at the Princess's to Mr. William Beverley. Then he wrote stories for the *Family Herald*, and drew pictures for the *Man in the Moon*. In 1851 he edited a Conservative magazine, and became the *fidus Achates* of Soyer, the illustrious cook, in connection with the Countess of Blessington's symposium, which forms part of the interesting history of the first Great Exhibition.

Even up to this date Mr. Sala had still to discover his *métier* in life, for his next position was that of a partner in an insurance and advertising agency. One evening he was accidentally locked out of his house. Walking the streets all night inspired him with a humorous sketch, entitled " The Key of the Street." He dropped this into the editorial box of *Household Words*, in which famous publication it promptly appeared. This was the beginning of his literary association with Charles Dickens, " but for whom," he says, " I should never have been a journalist or a writer of books. The first five-pound note I ever earned by literature came from his kind hand. He urged me to enter into the lists of journalism, and watched with interest my progress."

III.

And a very remarkable progress it was. Since 1851 his pen has been one of the brightest and busiest in what I venture to call literary journalism. Leader-writer, critic, correspondent, he has filled every position with a success that has never waned. In the midst of war and peace he has narrated the current history of his time in almost every land and on every sea. The marvel is that, outside all this extraordinary work, he has contributed articles to magazines and written many books.

His best-known works are "How I Tamed Mrs. Cruiser," "Twice Round the Clock," "A Journey Due North," "The Baddington Peerage," "Dutch Pictures, with some Sketches in the Flemish Manner," "Shipchandler, and other Tales," "Two Prima Donnas," "Breakfast in Bed," "Strange Adventures of Captain Dangerous," "After Breakfast," "Quite Alone," "A Trip to Barbary," "From Waterloo to the Peninsula," "Rome and Venice," "Paris Herself Again," and "America Re-visited." He was the special correspondent of the *Telegraph* in the United States in 1863. During the following year he described the Emperor's visit to Algeria. In 1870 he was at Metz, in Eastern France, for the same paper. Having witnessed the fall of the Empire, he went to Rome and recorded the entry of the Italian Army into the Eternal City. He was in Spain when Alfonso XII. made his royal entry into Madrid. Then he went to Venice and described the fêtes which celebrated the interview of the Emperor Francis Joseph and King Victor Emanuel. In 1876 he travelled from St. Petersburg to Moscow; thence to Warsaw; subsequently traversing the entire length of the Empire to tell the story of the mobilisation of the Russian Army. Reaching Odessa and Constantinople by the Black Sea, he was in time for the opening of the Conference on the Eastern Question, since which date he has done notable work in connection with other great European events from distant capitals. His letters from the United States, under the heading "America Re-visited," were for many weeks a leading attraction in the *Daily Telegraph*, which has since published his entertaining notes on Australia.

IV.

A busy man, Sala evidently finds his chief recreation in what most people would call hard work.

"Yes," he says, in reply to a suggestive question of mine in that direction, "I am never idle, and in the autumn of my life I think I find my chief pleasure in studying the technique of every trade and profession. You will feel this when you see the tools in my workshop. I had a little leisure at Brussels recently, and occupied myself in brushing up my knowledge of the Russian language. Here are my notes."

He handed me a small memorandum book with many very carefully written studies in the Russian character. I have often regarded myself as a hard

"HERE ARE MY NOTES."

worker, but Sala puts to the blush the most industrious of journalistic labourers.

V.

"I will not ask you," I say, as we adjourn to the library, "to what you attribute your great success as a journalist, because it is sufficiently apparent in your tools, your notes, your commonplace book, your industry, and your work; but it will interest some of my readers if you say a few words to me on this subject."

"The success of my career," he replies, "may be very briefly but emphatically set forth as follows:— First, I was educated abroad; I spoke French and Italian before I ever saw England. I was taught to draw from my earliest years. I served an apprenticeship as an engraver. I was a scene-painter at the Princess's Theatre, a caricaturist on the *Man in the Moon*, and consequently brought to my work, as a special correspondent and journalist, a variety of capacity not ordinarily found. They say 'Jack of all trades and master of none,' but you are no bad journeyman in journalism if you know the technicalities of a good many trades: and as I said before, I still keep up as earnestly as ever my studies of technique, and I buy every work of any importance or interest about every kind of trade. The stage, I need not say, has always been to me a delightful study. On the shelves near you, you will find a wonderful collection of plays —the best editions of Ben Jonson, one or two very old Shakespeares in their original bindings, all Goldoni's works, in a language as familiar to me as my own tongue. I never was a reporter; I came straight from the literary columns of *Household Words* into the editorial columns of the *Daily Telegraph*, being at the same time its art critic, frequently its operatic and dramatic critic, and its special correspondent in all parts of the world."

"Most of your work in this latter department of journalism has been, I think, despatched by mail; and in this respect it is no doubt a great compliment to be able to say that the electric telegraph has done very little to injure the current history of your letters."

"One tries," he says, "sometimes to write ahead of the cable; but I have done some long despatches by telegraph, notably seven columns of the coronation of Alexander III. I wrote that straightaway, with messengers at my elbow, and was almost surprised, and I need not say delighted, when I learned that it had got safely to headquarters. I think it was the next day that Mrs. Sala telegraphed to me: 'Messages safely arrived; seven columns.'"

VI.

"You have many friends," I say, "in the United States?"

"I think so. I used to have some enemies; but I was a correspondent, you know, during the war, and possibly felt more than I ought for the South. I think that was because my mother was a West Indian slave-owner, and I believe I hated the coloured gentlemen. My letters to the *Telegraph* in those days gave

Sir Edwin Arnold and his colleagues a good deal of anxiety. I think they hated them; for the North had no more devoted friend and ally than my chief and journalistic companion, Edwin Arnold, whose " Light of Asia" and other poems are, I am glad to know, very familiar and very popular in the United States. As for myself, I have reason to know and to be thankful for having many good friends in America, in spite of that little Southern sympathy I undoubtedly had in the days of the war. I have been there, as you know, several times since, and have been cordially received. My "Echoes of the Week," which I wrote for some years in the *Illustrated London News*, brought me a great deal of correspondence from all parts of the United States—inquiries, notes, complimentary messages, and other very friendly and interesting epistles."

IV.

AMERICANS IN LONDON.

First Experiences—"I shall have some funny things to tell them home"—Policemen, Cabs, and the Irish Question—"So Solid"—Winter's "Trip to England"—A Tribute to the Old Country—Reminiscences of Home the Spiritualist.

I.

"I THINK I have met you in Massachusetts?" said a newly-imported citizen of the Great Republic, as he stood by my side at a window of the American Exchange.

"Perhaps."

"You are an American?"

"No, unfortunately," I said, with a conciliatory smile.

"Well you may say that," replied my casual acquaintance; "though, mind you, there is plenty to admire in this country. I have only been here a week; most of that time I have spent at Westminster Abbey. We've got nothing of that kind home. That Westminster Abbey is a thing to be proud of, I tell you. But

OUR AMERICAN COUSIN.

what has astonished me most is your banking-houses;
must have been a thousand clerks in the one I
was at this morning, and they were shovelling the
gold about in scoops as if it was dirt. Never seen
so much money in my life as I see them chucking
about in that office; no, sir!"

II.

" In what vessel did you come over ? "

" The ' Umbria '; sick all the way; they gathered
round to see me die, but I concluded to come on. It
was a pretty bad storm, but 'safe, if slow,' is the
motto. Well, how do you manage to live here?
that's what I can't understand. Don't think I
could; but there's one thing that I like, that's the
civility you meet with. Now, in America, you
wouldn't have sat down and talked to me like this.
No, sir, you bet! I shall have some funny things
to tell them home. I see a notice about tickets,
and I asked for one to Cardiff, and he says, ' It's
a pound and two.' I give him two pound, and he
hands me the change. When I get into the depôt
I says, ' Where's the train ? ' ' Here,' says a sort of
policeman, pointing to a row of things like second-
hand coffins. ' The cars, I mean,' I answers, and he
says, ' Them's them.' So I says, ' Which for Cardiff ? '
And he says, ' This; are you booked ? ' and I says, ' No.'
' Then you can't go in unless you're booked,' he says,

and I began to think that I had neglected something in the way of papers, and would have to go to the American consul about it. 'That's very awkward,' I says. 'It would be very awkward for you if you got in and went on without being booked,' he answered, in a way that made me feel timid, and I began to think of the high-handed style you Britishers have of dealing with foreigners, and so I thought I would make a clean breast of the affair and tell him that I did not know what he meant; and he says, 'Come this way and I'll show you,' which, he being a big fellow and me a little one, as you see, and a stranger, rather increased my trepidation, and the weather so bad and all; but he only took me to the place where I had bought my ticket, and he says, 'There; that's the bookin' office,' and I says, 'What shall I do?' 'Why, take your ticket,' he says, and I answered that I had bought a ticket. 'Why didn't *you* say so afore?' he says, and I said, 'Why didn't you say so before?' and he says, 'I did ask you if you was booked, and you said "No"'; and then I laughed and told him I was an American and didn't understand, and then he laughed, and we had a drink, but the difference between what you call things and what we call them is wonderful."

III.

"Do you stay long in England?"

"Mean to stay till it's clear enough to see it—summer, I suppose, is fine—want to see your hedges and meadows in bloom, and something of the country. Your police is a grand system. Yesterday I calls a

"HI! CABBIE, YOU TAKE THAT FARE FOR TWO SHILLINGS."

hansom cab, and I says, 'What will you charge to drive me to Regent's Park?' and he says 'A crown.' Well, that's $1.25, which is nothing much for us with a cab, and I was getting in when a policeman standing on hand says, 'Hi! cabbie, you take that fare for 2s.; and if you try on this game again, and I see you, I'll have your licence withdrawn.' That would never have occurred in Boston or New York—a policeman interfering to see a person righted.* He drives me like mad to Regent's Park, and I gave him 2s., and I says, 'Here's an extra shilling for you if you'll walk that horse back,' and he says, 'All right.' I'm given to horses myself, and I don't like to see 'em ill-treated. I think of going to Ireland, and I'm surprised to hear so little about Ireland. Our people home jump to conclusions about these things. 'War sure,' they said, when I came away, and I expected to find all England up in arms, and I find London going ahead as if nothing was the matter. And a gentleman smiled at me in the smoking-room of the Golden Cross, and he said, 'Oh, it's nothing; they want to have the land given to them and not to pay any rent, and it can't be done'; and I said, 'I should think not.' Fact is, we don't understand these affairs on our side, until

---

* The London policemen are not so fine in their physique as our Chicago guardians—who, by the way, are probably the finest appearing body of men in the world. But the London policeman, although rarely a giant, has some compensating traits. He can be found occasionally when he is wanted. He is always civil when applied to for information. He is not hampered by interests of ward politics. In fine, his life is so arranged that he has some little time each day to devote to his business as a policeman. Upon the whole, I think he has an occasional point of superiority over the average policeman of the States.—*Sketches Beyond the Sea.*

we come over and study them for ourselves. Isn't it so?"

"ARE YOU BOOKED?"

"Yes," I answered, "it is a good thing for Americans and Englishmen to visit each other and form their own judgment upon international questions."

IV.

"It is surprising how civil everybody is—servants especially in the hotels. Home they chuck things at you, as much as to say, 'Take it or leave it.' Here

"YES, SIR,—NO, SIR."

it is 'Yes, sir,' and 'No, sir,' all the time, and I find it quite soothing. So far as I can see I don't know what the Irish have to complain of. Seems to me Englishmen are fair enough. Never was in a country that seems so solid—all your buildings solid, St.

Paul's and the railway depôts solid, cabs, omnibuses
solid, and I suppose it's solid under the mud and
slush of the streets when you get to the bottom. I
tell you there's a good deal to admire, and everybody
looks healthy—don't see the consumptive faces and
sunken eyes you see home; you take things easy, and
something is to be allowed for what you eat; and we
are so tarnation fast home—our climate does it, they
tell me. But, after all, home's home, and I couldn't
stand this fog—it's getting worse, I think—or has
my watch stopped?—no, it's half after three—hope
I'll see you again. It's very kind of you to sit down
and have a talk—it's worth $10 to come in and see
an American face—I would have bet $100 yours was
one. Well, good afternoon!"

V.

And so we parted, the stranger to continue his
experiences of English life, I to my club, where I jot
down this characteristic conversation, which contains
in a short space the genuine first impressions of a
middle-class citizen of the State of Massachusetts. A
great Spanish painter gave one lesson to his pupils,
"Go to Nature." In this simple sketch I have acted
upon his advice, and I hope the unconscious model will
not object to the result. It was pleasant to watch
his intelligent face, and the eagerness of his unsophisti-
cated eyes, as he gave me his account of learning the

meaning of being "booked," and to note the smile of superiority which spread over his pleasant face when he likened the London and North-Western Railway carriages to second-hand coffins.

VI.

Mr. Winter is on a visit to London. He spoke at a recent banquet on the relations between England and America. When Toole visited New York he welcomed him in some choice poetic stanzas; when Irving left he sent after him, over the sea, a tender poetic voice of farewell. Mr. Winter is the dramatic critic of the *Tribune*, and a sweet and tuneful poet. Among all the graceful tributes to England which have been published since Washington Irving's time, nothing more eloquent or touching has appeared than "A Trip to England," by this delightful lyrist and good fellow, Mr. William Winter. The volume is made up from letters contributed to the *New York Tribune*. They are issued this year in an *édition de luxe*, with illustrations by Mr. Joseph Jefferson, the actor, whose Rip Van Winkle is not more delicate in artistic finish than are his black-and-white sketches of London. In a brief preface to these letters we are told that "their writer passed ten weeks of the summer of 1887 in England and France, where he met with a great and surprising kindness, and where he saw many beautiful and memorable things," the desire to commemorate which led to the republication of this *Tribune* correspondence. The volume needs no apology. The beauties of England, and the sympathetic language that the poet finds in her gurgling streams, her song-birds, her whispering woods, and in the echoes of her gray cathedrals and moss-grown ruins of ancient hall and castle, find a deep and fervent expression in Mr. Winter's book. As witness :—

"England contains many places like Windsor; some that blend, in even richer amplitude, the elements of quaintness, loveliness, and magnificence. The meaning of them all is, as it seemed to me, the same: that romance, and beauty, and gentleness are not effete, but for ever vital; that their forces are within our own souls, and ready and eager to find their way into all our thoughts, actions, and circumstances, and to brighten for every one of us the face of every day; that they ought rather to be relegated to the distant and the past, not kept for our books and day-dreams alone; but—in a calmer and higher mood than is usual in this age of universal mediocrity, critical scepticism, and miscellaneous tumult—should be permitted to flow out into our architecture, adornments, and customs, to hallow and preserve our antiquities, to soften our manners, to give us tranquillity, patience, and tolerance, to make our country lovable for our own hearts, and so to enable us to bequeath it, sure of love and reverence, to succeeding ages."

VII.

Mrs. Home, I see, has been writing a life of her late husband. I knew him intimately. Some years ago he was a constant visitor at a little country-house of mine. The late Dr. Phillip Williams and the Rev. Digby Cotes, of Worcester, met him there, as did also Mr. Sherriff, the late member for Worcester, the late Mark Lemon, and others. He had *carte blanche* to astonish us with manifestations of his powers, but he never at any time availed himself of the opportunity to make converts of us. He was an accomplished young man, and an agreeable and amiable guest; but he could call no spirits from the vasty deep when he was at my house. During the famous suit, which he met honourably by paying into court the money that had been settled upon him, he called one morning to ask my advice upon a particular question that had arisen on the previous day. "If you possess the supernatural power you claim," I said, "give the court an example of it. You floated in and out of the windows in Victoria Street; to-morrow morning sail round the Court of Queen's Bench, tweak the nose of the foreman of the jury, flick off the judge's wig, make the place resound with wild knockings, send banjoes and accordions on excursions about the heads of barristers and lawyers, and make yourself generally and obnoxiously known." He appeared to be somewhat

offended at my levity, and we never met again. The
late Czar of All the Russias received him on a later
occasion with much consideration, which should have
fully compensated him for any want of appreciation of
his spiritualistic powers on the part of so humble an
individual as myself. His book of "Confessions" is
as startling a collection of ghost stories as can be
found in modern literature, and many of them are
"authenticated" by witnesses. Dr. Gully, of Malvern,
was a great spiritualist; so, also, was Mr. S. C. Hall,
the veteran author and founder of the *Art Journal*.

V.

LITERARY MEN AND ACTORS.

Fox is of Opinion that Literary Men and Actors should not Marry — Actresses' Husbands — The old Fashion — Lady Beaconsfield, Mrs. Gladstone, and other Famous Wives — Shrews and Helpmates.

I.

"And I cannot help thinking, nevertheless," remarks Fox, as he crosses his legs in my favourite arm-chair, "that literary men and actors should not marry."

"Why?" I ask.

AN AFTER-DINNER CHAT.

"Oh, not for their own sakes, but for the sake of the women."

But again I ask, "Why?"

"Because they are a wretched self-conscious lot—literary men and actors."

"Thank you," I say.

"Present company excepted, of course; you never obtrude your work, as it seems to me, upon your family. But look at our friend So-and-So the novelist; when he is at work he maintains a dead silence for days together; he is busy with his fictitious characters; they are with him more or less from morning till night. When he is writing the house must be still as the grave; his luncheon is put through a trap-door. And our friend Aristides the actor, he does not get up until lunch-time; then he is overwhelmed with letters."

"Mostly begging letters," I suggest.

"Well, no matter," says Fox, "he has no leisure for domestic chat; he must go out into the air a little, though his wife has not time just then to accompany him; then he must have his light dinner; and after a necessary sleep he must be off to the theatre and act; goes to his club to sup, gets home—well, your own wife can tell us what time he gets home, by making a note of the late hours which you keep occasionally."

"Then how should these poor fellows live?" I ask the diplomatic and Scotland-yard philosopher.

"Ah! that is another question; I know if I were a woman, not the most prosperous of the poor fellows, as you call them, would get me for a wife. I repeat, literary men and actors should not marry."

II.

"Then what about literary women and actresses?"

LATE HOURS.

"An entirely different matter; they should marry. If they make plenty of money, they should marry; if they do not, they should marry. If they are well-off in their work, they want a good fellow to take care of them; if they are not, they want an equally good fellow to prevent them from going on and making fools of themselves."

"But actresses' husbands, as a rule, are not considered very good fellows, eh? Often marry to be kept, eh? I have heard that said."

"Oh, yes, and sometimes it is true, just as it is true about men who marry heiresses. There are many exceptions. Look at So-and-So, whose wife writes books and he works them; never was a more honest or satisfactory partnership. Look at So-and-So, whose wife acts and he manages her; that's all right. And then the non-artistic husband has a better time than the non-artistic wife; a man can keep a woman in order where a woman can't keep a man's temper in check."

"But 'it goes ill with the house where the hen crows,' is a good proverb," I remark.

"It does not apply in these days, where woman's right to be a bread-winner is acknowledged."

III.

"It is not a natural partnership; the old fashion is surely the best. The man goes out and hunts and fights, brings home the food; the wife stays behind to keep things in order, and look to the pot; the man the protector; the woman the loving dependent, the solacer, the comforter."

"All very well in the hunting days," Fox replies, "when the life was what Nature intended, in the fields and the woods; the man going forth to bring in food, the wife being the cook; the man strong-armed, heroic, brave, and admired by the women for these qualities. The woman in our artificial life admires long, lank hair, effeminate poses, pallid cheeks, dreamy eyes, and a lolloping so-called æsthetic gait; and the woman who can earn money upon the stage, or by writing books or painting pictures, occasionally, I think, likes to keep and protect this kind of degenerate thing called an artistic person."

"You are hard on our civilisation, Fox."

"On the contrary, it is hard on me."

IV.

"Do you not know how much Disraeli owed to the devotion and intellectual and practical alliance of his wife, as friend and partner?"

"Oh, yes," Fox replies, "and I remember that when Bishop Cooper was at work on his Lexicon, his wife in a fit of ill-temper cast a volume of his manuscript to the flames, and destroyed the labour of years."

"Let us come to the days in which we live. Had ever author or politician a better helpmate than has fallen to the lot of Mr. Gladstone?"

"History is as good for illustration as the news of the moment," Fox answers with a snap; "Goethe was cursed with a shrew, and Steele's wife hurried him to an untimely end."

"Since you prefer ancient to modern history," is

my answer, "I give you the wife of Wieland the poet, whose gentle good sense and docility were of great assistance to him in his work, and with whom he spent happy days; if there was rain, there was always

THE BISHOP AND HIS LEXICON.

sunshine to follow. My dear friend, turn to Disraeli's 'Literary Character,' and you will find that the records of women, happy with literary husbands, are in the majority. Wives need not be the votaries of the men of genius, but they may be their faithful companions. In the character of the higher female, Disraeli says we may discover a constitutional faculty of docility and enthusiasm which has varied with the genius of different ages. 'It is the opinion of an eminent metaphysician, that the mind of the female adopts and familiarises itself with ideas more easily than that of man, and hence the facility with which the sex contract or lose habits, and accommodate their minds to new situations. Politics, war, and learning are equally objects of attainment to their delightful susceptibility.' And then he gives instances of the way in which women have flung themselves into the arts which their husbands loved, and been of conspicuous service and obtained distinction thereby. Take Buffon, who said to a friend, 'Often when I cannot please myself and am impatient at the disappointment, Madame de Buffon reanimates my exertion or withdraws me to repose for a short interval; I return to my pen refreshed and aided by her advice.' Gesner confessed, and delighted in the confession, that whatever his talents were, the person who had most contributed to develop them was his wife. 'Imagine a woman,' says Disraeli, 'attending to the domestic economy and to the commercial details, yet withdrawing out of this business of life into the more elevated pursuits of her husband; and at the same time combining with all this the cares and counsels which she bestowed on her son to form the artist and the man.' If one might drop into mere personal gossip of the day, I could give you as great an example of this in a humbler sphere perhaps ; to-day I know a wife who has done all this, and does it now ; though her will is stronger than her physical power, a wife who manages her house, keeps the banking account, takes personal interest in the work of her artistic family, sometimes inspires it, and by her care, taste, devotion, and self-sacrifice, has an acknowledged share in the successes of her husband and their children."

IV.

THE BATTLE OF LONDON.

The Story of Sir Augustus Harris—A Business Man—Earnestness and Energy—Audacity—Difficulty—The Fight—A Walk in the Park—Ups and Downs—Success—Stage-Work, Past, Present and French.

I.

In these days of "Reminiscences," there is no career in either art, politics, or literature that does not seem to be of special interest. As I have said before, however, it must be a career in which there has been a fight, and the biographer must be of importance in the world's estimation. Some time ago, when I was commissioned by a great syndicate of American journals to write a series of "Chats with Celebrities," I selected, as an interesting example of courage and enterprise in theatrical management, the lessee of Drury Lane.

The fact that since the present sketch first appeared Mr. Harris has filled the honoured office of Sheriff of the City of London, with its pleasant sequel of knighthood, adds a new interest to this remarkable story of a remarkable career.

The story of Harris's siege and capture of Drury Lane is quite a romance in its way, and will be as notable a story fifty years hence as it is now. Men's fights in the battle of London, particularly their victories, are always more or less impressive: the campaigner's ground is so difficult, the nerve required so exceptional, the victory when it is won so well worth the winning.

II.

"Yes," he said, "Drury Lane is the largest, the most expensive, and I suppose the most famous of the historic theatres in London. I am its lessee and manager, and during my first six years of management, I was one of its attractions as an actor. That is something for a fellow under forty to say without boasting, is it not?"

"It is," I replied.

"Mind you," he went on, "I know that some people think it vain and not altogether in good taste that I should advertise myself so much. If I were conceited I should be disturbed at this expression of opinion; but I am not conceited. I am a business man; I have a policy and I follow it out. Why should I expend my money and labour in advertising Drury Lane all the time, or devote my life to making the fortune of some star who may become my master? No; I advertise Augustus Harris, making Augustus Harris as worthy of public favour as I can; and there is this advantage in being your own star—you know that you can depend upon yourself. Look at the Gyes! They have lived to make Adelina Patti. Where are they? Nowhere. On the other hand, look at Rosa. He kept himself and his work to the front—Carl Rosa's Opera Company—and he was Carl Rosa all over the world. Now, don't you imagine that I am going to compare myself with Irving, but he is a grand modern example of a manager being his own star; and while I repeat I am a modest man with a policy, I will say this for myself, that, emulating the example of Irving in his artistic production of the poetic drama, and of the Bancrofts in their mounting of comedy, I feel that I may fairly take the credit of doing for spectacular plays and for pantomimes, that which they have done for what is called the higher drama. In regard to pantomime, I have put into it every known art that can be pressed into the service of the stage—painting, dressing, decoration, music; and I look back with pride and with pleasure upon some of the fairy and realistic scenes of Drury Lane under my management.'

III.

As the manager of Drury Lane talked to me, I realised to the full the graphic description of him, written by one of the accomplished authors of "Celebrities at Home," in Edmund Yates's *World*. "You never met a man who gives himself up more entirely to any task he has in hand than Augustus Harris. Peculiarly rapid in thought, he always conveys the impression of a man who fears that he will not be able to communicate his ideas with sufficient exactitude. He tries to speak with his eyes, his hands, his shoulders, his knees, as well as his lips." This is a special tribute to his earnestness and his energy, for he holds under full control an excitable temperament. He is a young man, looks older than his years, is broad in build, of medium height; just the physique for the British naval officer in Fawcett Rowe's *Freedom*, a drama which, with a little revision and more compactness of construction, should bear revival. I had breakfasted with "Gusaris" (as one of the foreign critics styles him), at his rooms in Portland Place. I had strolled through the very handsome apartments, admired their Japanese decorations, noted their owner's unique collection of books on costumes, his interesting library of Continental authors (Harris is a linguist), his store of old Covent Garden prompt books (his father was the well-known manager of the Italian Opera in its palmy days), and we had adjourned to his study to smoke, when the conversation I am recording commenced.

IV.

"And now tell me," I said, "if you will, under what circumstances you took Drury Lane Theatre. The public will, I am sure, appreciate the energy and courage of the beginning of that enterprise, the success of which justifies what we may call the audacity of it."

"Yes," he exclaims, with a roar of laughter, "it was audacious."

"Do you mind telling me the story?"

"No, not at all," he says, with that anxious expression in his face which the *World* writer noticed, but followed with another sudden peal of laughter. "It is only a few years ago, but I couldn't do it now. Some people think I have plenty of impudence——"

This with another roar of laughter.

"But I couldn't do that again! Well, this is how I became manager of Drury Lane Theatre. You must know that when I was a mere boy I was an actor of small parts in the provinces, became a member of Barry Sullivan's company, and had got a good deal

of experience under my father and in other directions.
I was with Col. Mapleson for three years at Drury
Lane, and—like my cheek, you'll say—always thought
I could improve on his method of working the theatre.
Well, soon after that I was Edgar Bruce's stage

manager at the Royalty. Things were not going
well, and I suggested doing a little show-piece, a
burlesque called *Venus*; we did it, and it was a
great success. But I will come back to that. Drury
Lane under Chatterton had been going to the bad, and
Covent Garden was not doing much better. When

Chatterton's lease was up, I put in, among other candidates for it, a speculative offer. No go, and perhaps it was as well, for I had very hazy notions as to how I should raise the money. In less than a year, as I was passing the theatre, I found a notice on the walls that it was closed. Chatterton was beaten. Well, I had always thought I could work Drury Lane, and I felt sure that properly done, well done, it was a certainty; my main idea being pantomime on the very highest scale of art.'

v.

" You know, perhaps," I said, " that pantomime is not known in America on the English lines. They would, I fancy, regard it as a variety entertainment idealised—a spectacular fairy drama with comic breaks in it; something between humorous opera and fairy extravaganza."

"And that is the kind of work it really is! Do you think they have ever seen anything on as grand a scale as my procession of kings and queens in *Sinbad the Sailor?*"

" I don't think they have," I said, " nor anything as striking as your Lord Mayor's Show. But don't let me interrupt you."

" Well, I had made a little success, as I say, with Bruce; he paid me a salary of £5 a week. A gentleman there, a Mr. K., who was joint capitalist with

Bruce, was delighted with what I had done, and on that very night of the closing of Drury Lane, said he would like to take a theatre on his own account. I at once laid my ideas about Drury Lane before him. 'Take it,' he said, 'I will find you all the money you want.' I saw the committee of Drury Lane proprietors, and after some negotiations, to which my youthfulness was for a time somewhat of a bar, they agreed to accept me as a tenant, and I was to pay £1000 down. Full of joy, I went to Mr. K., and to cut this part of the story short, let me say that he was *non est*."

VI.

Here Harris rose from his seat to laugh and walk about, and then to pause and look me full in the face, with the exclamation:—

"I had got the theatre, but not the money! I was the new and accepted lessee of the National Theatre, entitled to a military guard at night, and all that sort of thing, and all the money I had in the world was exactly £3 15s. I went to B., who said he would help me only he couldn't for various reasons; but would I go down to the Aquarium, have lunch, and talk it out. I was in the humour to go anywhere, to catch at any straw. At the Aquarium he introduced me to a Mr. Rendell, in these words: 'Allow me to introduce my friend, Mr. Augustus Harris, the

SIR AUGUSTUS HARRIS.

new lessee of Drury Lane. I believe you were one of the unsuccessful proposers for the theatre?' Then turning to me, he said: 'Mr. Rendell wanted to give the Vokeses a chance at the Lane.' The result of that accidental introduction was that I invited Rendell to join forces with me. I was perfectly frank with him, told him how I was situated, that my worldly

means were represented by a balance at my bank of
£3 15s., but that I never had a financial transaction
of which I need be ashamed; that I was poor, but
honest, as they say in the play, and the rest of it. I
offered him all the security for his money he would
take, and his own terms as to sharing. I saw him
several times, and told him that with £3000 I
would undertake to open the theatre, and produce
my pantomime. This was a bold venture, no doubt,
seeing that at the moment Covent Garden, the rival
house, had a backer, and was going to do pantomime
on the most lavish scale. A bold venture! I look
back, and it seems madness. Well, sir, I think
Rendell got tired of me, and to get rid of me at last
said: 'Look here, Harris, I will find the £3000, on
condition that you find £1000—the first £1000 of
the necessary £3000.' I said: 'I'll do it.'"

VII.

Then my host laughed aloud, lighted a fresh cigar,
and, thus refreshed, resumed his interesting narrative:

"In connection with the lease of a theatre, as you
know, there is a refreshment contract. You let off
the refreshment bars. I went to Dodsworth and
let him the refreshment contract for £250; then by
dint of some pressure I got a relation to do a little
bill for £250, and then for the life of me I did not
see my way any further. That afternoon I took a

walk in the park, meditating on the failure which stared me in the face.

"'Ah, Gussy,' said a voice, 'looking thoughtful: do the cares of management come so soon?'

"I turned round and met a couple of friends. They congratulated me on my new position. I told them I had not quite concluded the contract, but hoped to do so. They asked me to go home to dinner with them. I did, wondering whether I should ask them to lend me the £500. I concluded after dinner that they would perhaps be frightened at £500; but might be induced to lend £250. Over a cigar I told them my story, and added their £250 to the rest, and the next day I bounced into Rendell's office with the declaration, 'Got £750 — can't get any more!' My frankness, my earnestness, more than my plans, I think, won him, and he became my partner, but the capital

MEDITATION.

was £2750, not £3000. The next day I paid the £1000, to the great delight of the Drury Lane lawyers, and to the very great surprise of my own!"

VIII.

Another hearty laugh, and the narrative went on :

"Seventeen hundred and fifty pounds to carry the theatre up to Christmas, and produce the pantomime —and to fight Covent Garden, with its new capital and its previous year's success, which had practically burst up Drury Lane! Rignold applied to me to let him have the theatre to produce *Henry V.* I agreed, counting on this to give me breathing time—and something towards the rent—for the pantomime; though it was no joke to mount *Henry V.* and get the pantomime ready also. Beverley, the scene painter, the life and soul it was thought, and properly, of Drury Lane, received my instructions to prepare for these two events with a cynical laugh, said I was 'a young ass—an idiot,' etc., and chucked up his position.

"Here was a go! But I was not to be done. I telegraphed to all the scene painters whom I knew, set several of them to work, never rested night or day until I got things into shape, never allowed anybody else to rest, worked like a nigger; so did everybody. *Henry V.* was successfully produced. I got my staff together for the pantomime of *Blue Beard*. At the end of the season I found myself with a credit at the bank of £1000, and £1000 due for rent! And ten months to the next Christmas pantomime! A tight place, eh? However, Rendell stuck to me, and another friend came in. We produced *Madame Angot*, and at the end of this season were £3000 to the bad. In the meantime, I was getting ready the spectacular drama of *The World*, with Pettitt. But the loss of £3000 settled my backers, and I was once more left alone. I struggled on, however, announced *The World*, and had it ready for production when Rendell rejoined me. *The World* was a great success, and I have never looked back since."

IX.

"Now, will you give me a few figures to illustrate success or failure at Drury Lane?"

"Well, business that would mean prosperity at most other theatres would mean failure at Drury Lane. An ordinary Drury Lane success would mean a loss— the lessee of Drury Lane must have a big success every year to come out right. Last year's pantomime, as advertised, cost me £30,000 for 100 performances. I placed my books in the hands of Cooper Bros., the chartered accountants, and they certified to £29,000, demurring to £1000 as more personal than pantomime expenses. So that the cost was £290 each performance, or £600 a-day; and so you see what a

tremendous responsibility it is, and what a frost would
mean. My receipts have been £1000 a day, and they
have been down as low as £550. Many weeks I have
had as much as £500 and £900 below expenses. It
takes great items of profit to pull this back again;
and, however successful a piece, you are pretty sure to
drop down at the end of a long run. This one thing
is certain in these days, you must put plays or pantomime, or whatever you do, on the stage better than
they have ever been done before. American managers
are just beginning, I hear, to find this out. Once the
public see and understand a good thing they will not
be content with slip-shod work, or what is called
economical management. I think I have done my
work better every year. In my procession of kings
and queens in *Sinbad* there were 300 different costume
designs, and 650 people on the stage. The procession alone cost me £5000. Pantomime is not considered high art. It is my ambition to make it so.
Without egotism, I consider that there is nothing
much more artistic possible in the way of ballet than
my ballet scene in this present pantomime. France
has nothing to show within a thousand miles of it. I
have just come from Paris, and am intimately acquainted with the French stage. To-day, Paris is
behind us in everything theatrical. She has a few
big actors, it is true, and two or three great dramatists,
notably Sardou and Dumas; but take the average,

and our actors are better, our pieces are better mounted, our theatres are better, our stage art is higher and of

BEHIND THE SCENES.

more earnest and sincere intention. They are doing pieces now in Paris the mounting of which would have been hissed in London, and the acting of which would not have been applauded."

X.

" What are your greatest Drury Lane successes ? "

" *Youth, The World,* and *Whittington and his Cat.*"

As he says " good-bye " to me his wife brings the baby to be kissed, and Harris drives off to Drury Lane.

It should encourage disappointed young fellows who are struggling with fortune, this simple sketch of Sir Augustus Harris's capture of Drury Lane. But in emulating his energy and audacity they must not forget that he is a worker. Genius is often only another name for industry. Harris never tires. He can work all day and all night if necessary. There is a tired expression in his face and manner, perhaps; but never in his labour, nor in his ambition, which is centred in the one idea of managerial prosperity, with as much art as can be got into it. If he has some of the instinct of Mr. Barnum in the way of advertising, he inherits his father's taste, and he takes a genuine pride in artistic stage management. When his father died, in 1873, his effects were sold, and many of them at heavy prices. Now that his son has means, he loses no opportunity to purchase them back. Among his most valued treasures, and not the least interesting of his collection, are mementos of his father and his Covent Garden career. If a man's mind is reflected in his surroundings, Sir Augustus Harris might be content to be judged by his artistic home at Portland Place.

XI

Since this chat for that series of articles for America about successful men and celebrities, the Drury Lane manager has gone on his managerial way rejoicing, producing each year a fresh pantomime more gorgeous and successful than the last, acting no longer himself, but sharing in the dramatic construction of several plays that have held his stage in the intervals of pantomime, and increased the balance at his bankers. His "leisure" has been occupied in starting Masonic Lodges, fighting an election for the onerous post of County Councillor, and winning his way to the Shrievalty; his theatrical triumphs have been supplemented by victories in connection with the lyric stage. His ambition in regard to opera, it seems, was slumbering when we had that long-ago chat, to break out comparatively recently in a vigorous effort to revive Italian Opera, and to do it at Drury Lane. He flung himself into the business with characteristic energy,

SIR AUGUSTUS AT HOME.

gave the town a season of excellent work, and lost by the adventure, it is said, £20,000; but nothing daunted, he went on, took Covent Garden, a far more legitimate house for opera than Drury Lane, and began his labours this time with a preliminary subscription for boxes and seats, which secured the financial success of his season. Under his management Italian Opera, after several years of retrogression, has come up again as a fashionable entertainment, and Covent Garden, under Harris, has never seen more distinguished audiences—and the productions have been worthy of the subscribers. The Gyes are entirely eclipsed, and one is sorry to see Mr. Mapleson, the prince of opera managers, struggling in the competition to hold some kind of a place. It is hardly possible that two great Opera Houses can be made to pay, even in our wealthy city of London; but one must wish Mr. Mapleson success for Auld Lang Syne, out of respect to his wonderful pluck and out of sympathy for his wonderful struggles. What an interesting account of all his ups and downs, and the difficulties of the life of an operatic *impresario*, he has written!

But to return to Sir Augustus, the subject of this present after-dinner chat. He has left Portland Place to live in a pretty corner of the Regent's Park region, a neighbour of that "Queen of Bohemia" whom the dear old Vicar in the story admired so much that one of my readers informed me he half thought I meant to marry his reverence to the red-haired beauty. Mr. Harris did not, you see, stand outside Drury Lane, vowing melodramatic vows to be the lessee and manager of that once very white elephant ; but he laid his plans for the siege, sat down before the citadel with the invading army of his wit and audacity, and now he is—well, they say from the County Council he is invited to go into Parliament. It is in no spirit of disparagement to Sir Augustus Harris, nor to any other County Councillor in particular, when I confess that it does not strike me as a hopeful addition to our legislative assemblies, if the County Council is to be regarded as a kind of stepping-stone to St. Stephen's.

VII.

"THE STAR OF SOUTH AFRICA."

A word with the *Cornhill*—The Koh-i-noor and the "Porter Rhodes"—Off-colour—The Beginning of Diamond Mining at the Cape—"O'Reilly's Folly"—Fever—A Note of Comfort—And otherwise.

I.

RECENTLY I came across an article on "Diamonds," in the *Cornhill Magazine*. It was capitally written, showed a knowledge of the subject, and was apt in the way of anecdote and illustration. The writer not only did not quote me, but he rather slurred over a book entitled "Great Diamonds of the World" (by Mr. Streeter and a *collaborateur*), which I edited. As an instance of the romance of to-day being equal in exciting episodes to the romance of the past, the article in the *Cornhill* told the story of a stolen diamond and the capture of the thief. That story was nothing more than a newspaper record of the time—a police report. I had found the facts in a Cape of Good Hope paper, and I turned them into a dramatic narrative for "Great Diamonds of the World." The *Cornhill* writer has set me thinking about diamonds, and there are a few points in my notes, connected with the work in question, which seem to me worth printing. At the same time, let me add, that I am making no charge of unfairness or plagiarism against my *Cornhill* friend; his well-written and admirably descriptive article is none the worse that myself and a Cape newspaper had inspired the central motive of it; but it is always an excellent plan to quote your sources of information; for, after all, treatment is the great thing in a magazine article. The world is so full of facts that the reader chiefly asks for a pleasant, and, if possible, a new setting of them when the medium is a newspaper or a magazine.

II.

The story of the Koh-i-noor is a remarkable romance. Its history would, fully told, be a record of the most startling incidents of Eastern intrigue and warfare. It was presented, as you know, by the East India Company to Her Majesty the Queen, and was recut by the advice of the late Prince Consort. It is more remarkable for its history than for its beauty, although it ranks in the first class of splendid gems. Mr. Porter Rhodes, who came over from the Cape of Good Hope with one of the largest "finds" in modern diamonds, waited upon the Queen to show her his African gem. She examined it with great interest and curiosity, and gave him and some friends a special order to inspect the Koh-i-noor at Windsor. The African diamond is evidently a far purer stone than the Koh-i-noor. It has, however, of course, the disadvantage of being at present uncut. Mr. Streeter and a syndicate of London diamond merchants offered Porter Rhodes £50,000 for the stone. He declined it, however, with surprising promptitude, and expected to receive double that sum. From my recent reading and some little experience in regard to gems, I do not hesitate to say that the London syndicate would refuse to-day to repeat their offer. No matter how expert a man may be in his judgment of diamonds in the rough, there is always serious danger of cleavage and other troubles. Some stones have literally broken up on the cutter's wheel.* There is no evidence in the "Porter Rhodes" diamond that anything serious in this direction would happen, but there is always a risk, and what is more, at the present moment news is continually arriving from the South African fields of the discovery of great stones.

III.

Diamond-mining is being prosecuted with so much scientific skill and vigour at the Cape that great stones promise no longer to be the rarity they were. The Empress Eugénie, who also inspected the Porter Rhodes diamond, expressed great surprise that it was

---

* The "Porter Rhodes" has recently been successfully cut, and is said to be a most brilliant and perfect tone.

not yellow. The Cape diamonds, as you know, have a reputation for being " off-colour," but latterly stones have been found equal in whiteness and purity to Brazilian gems. Within the past few months several finds of the greatest importance are known to have taken place at the Cape. One evening, not long ago, Mr. B. W. Murray read before the Society of Arts a most interesting and remarkable paper upon this subject. I venture to recall the main incidents which he narrated. They were reported in the society's journal, and were further exploited in " Great Diamonds of the World "; and, between ourselves, they are the foundation of episodical incidents in a certain novel called " The Gay World."

IV.

It was in 1867 that Mr. John O'Reilly, a trader and hunter, was passing through a portion of the British colony known as Griqualand West. At that time, however, the territory had not been ceded to the English Crown—it was under the chieftainship of Nicholas Waterboer. Albania was the particular district of the Griqua territory in which Mr. O'Reilly's adventure occurred. He was returning from the interior to Colesberg, and called upon a leading colonist, a Dutchman, one Mr. Van Niekirk, who entertained him hospitably. During the evening one of Niekirk's children was playing on the floor with some pebbles that had been gathered from the neighbourhood of the Vaal River. They were sparkling and attractive-looking things, and Mr. O'Reilly's attention was directed to one of them, which threw out quite a strong light. He took it up, examined it, and offered to buy it. Van Niekirk was amused at the idea of O'Reilly wishing to purchase the pebble, and refused to take any money for it. He told the traveller that he was quite welcome to take it. O'Reilly, in reply, informed him that he believed the pebble to be a precious stone of value, and he would therefore not take it for nothing. After some pleasant higgling between the two honest fellows, it was agreed that O'Reilly should take the stone, find out its value, and if it proved to be a diamond, as O'Reilly suspected, he was to sell it and divide the money between them.

MR. JOHN O'REILLY.

V.

O'Reilly took the stone to Colesberg, and at the bar of the local hotel showed it to several people and told them he believed it was a diamond. He cut a glass tumbler, and wrote his name upon the window-pane with it, and was laughed at even for these illustrations of his belief in its character.

DISCUSSED AT THE BAR.

One of the men present grew quite annoyed with O'Reilly's "folly," and, picking the stone up, threw it into the street. It was only after a long search that

O'Reilly found the stone again. He sent it to Dr. Atherton, of Grahamstown. This gentleman handed it over to the Roman Catholic Bishop, who was not only a theologian, but a scientist. He examined it, and unhesitatingly pronounced it to be a diamond of $22\frac{1}{2}$ carats. From Grahamstown the stone was forwarded to the Colonial Secretary, the Hon. Richard Southey, afterwards the Lieutenant-Governor of Griqualand West. He submitted the stone to the best authorities at hand, and they endorsed the judgment of the Bishop. It was then sent to Messrs. Hunt and Roskell, of London, the Queen's jewellers. They confirmed the decisions obtained in the colony, and valued the stone at £500. Sir Philip Wodehouse, who was Governor of the Colony at the time, purchased it at this valuation. Mr. O'Reilly thereupon set out on a fresh journey, to see if he could find other diamonds where this was picked up. He was fortunate in coming upon one of 8·78 carats, which was purchased by Sir Philip Wodehouse for £200. This was the beginning of the excitement which was caused by the opening of the diamond fields of South Africa, an excitement almost equal to that which followed the announcements of the discoveries of gold in Australia and California.

VI.

The diamond fever extended in all directions; it caught even the natives, who came swarming in from all parts with pebbles of all descriptions, many of them proving to be small diamonds. Soon afterwards the startling intelligence went through the country that a diamond of over 83 carats had been discovered. The story was quite true. Mr. Van Niekirk, hearing that the stone he had given to O'Reilly was a diamond, remembered that he had seen one of a similar character in the possession of a native. He went straight to the Kaffir, and found that the man still held possession of the stone in question. Van Niekirk bought it from him. The native, however, was a very cute native; he obtained from Van Niekirk five hundred sheep, a number of horses, and, indeed, almost the whole of the stock the Dutchman possessed. Van Niekirk, immediately on securing it, set off with the stone to Messrs. Lilienfield Brothers, of Hopetown, merchants of long standing in South Africa. They purchased the stone for £10,000, and christening it "The Star of South Africa," sent it to Messrs. Hunt and Roskell, of London, who eventually sold it to the late Lord Dudley, who had it set with ninety-five smaller brilliants, and it is still worn on important occasions by his beautiful widow.

A DIAMOND STUD.

VII.

From the moment of their discovery, through centuries, down to their latest possessors, the celebrated diamonds of the East have travelled through blood and adventure of the most dramatic character. Wars have been fought for them, children have been slain for them, monarchs have had their eyes put out for them, princes have been racked for them, and there is hardly a phase of torture invented by cruel despots which is not illustrated in the stories of lovely gems. It might even be noted, though one would be inclined to put it forward with great delicacy, and, of course, without for a moment implying one's belief in the Eastern superstition, that the Koh-i-noor brought ill-luck to the Queen. This stone, of all others, has had a career of misfortune. It was only a year or two after the Prince Consort placed it upon the cutter's wheel to have it re-shaped that he died, and Her Majesty has since then had some severe afflictions. Taken in connection with the previous history of the Koh-i-noor these are, to say the least, remarkable coincidences, although it would be folly to put them forward as examples of the theories which are soberly discussed in Eastern literature in regard to the supernatural powers of precious stones.

VIII.

As a note of comfort and reassurance to the diamond-loving readers of these papers, it is only fair to say that ill-luck is not traceable to the possession of small gems, such as are generally worn—to be particular let me say to the extent of 20 or 30 carats. I should be sorry to make any gentleman with a diamond in his shirt-front, or any lady with a pair in her ears, unhappy, and, therefore, add this supplementary exception in regard to the misfortunes that attend great diamonds. At present America does not possess a single historic stone. This is rather remarkable, considering how large a buyer she is in the diamond market. Seeing that without a break the histories of all the great gems are full of misadventure for those who touch them, perhaps Columbia is to be congratulated that all the famous stones are in Europe or Asia. No prejudice has, however, that I have heard of, grown up against big diamonds, though opals are regarded by even sensible people with superstitious fear. They are, nevertheless, favourite gems with the present Royal family of England. I recall a curious coincidence in connection with opals. An explorer from Costa Rica came home with a lot of opals. I and some friends bought several fine examples. I had mine set in a ring. One night, going home late, I presented this as a peace-offering to my wife. "Opals," I said, "are reputed unlucky: if you are superstitious throw the ring out of the window."

"I am not," she said; "what possible influence can a jewel have upon events? I laugh at such folly!"

She did not laugh the next morning. At 4.50, before daylight, our house was torn to pieces (and we narrowly escaped with our lives) by the explosion of five tons of gunpowder and other combustibles under our very windows. I had carried the opals home the night before "the Regent's Park explosion" of unhappy memory.

VIII.

CHARLES READE, AND "NABOTH'S VINEYARD."

Reade's Favourite Home—"A Dramatist by Natural Gift a Novelist by Force of Circumstances"—The Private Bill Demon—"Readiana"—From Albert Gate to Knightsbridge—"And I got Five Pounds for it"—Gardening and Literature—Wilkie Collins at Home—"Walker."

I.

DRIVING TO CHARLES READE'S HOME.

COME with me and I will show you the house that was "Naboth's Vineyard," the favourite London home of the late Charles Reade, possibly the strongest and most dramatic of all modern novelists. We take a hansom and drive along Piccadilly, past Hyde Park corner, to Knightsbridge. A cosy-looking house, one of a row, the front covered with creepers. If you turn to "A Terrible Temptation" you will find a full description of the internal economy of it. I do not propose to offer you a competitive picture, though I frequently had the pleasure of talking with the late Charles Reade and seeing him at work. There was no more conscientious writer. He once said to me, "I read two hundred books to write one," and more than once he has also said, "I am a dramatist by natural gift, and a novelist by force of circumstances," or words to that effect. When an official and officious effort was made to deprive Mr. Reade of his house he called it "Naboth's Vineyard," and secured, not only his own property, but the whole terrace, by the newspaper sermons which he preached from that text. Apart from his novels and plays, which need no praise from me (some of them are already accepted English classics), he devoted his pen to the public service in many directions. His publisher, Mr. Chatto, induced him shortly before his death to print a volume of selections from his newspaper letters under the characteristic title of "Readiana."

II.

If you will turn over the London newspaper files of 1883, you will find a controversy about "Private Bill legislation," which excited much attention at the time.

The reason for this was the discovery of a scheme, deftly laid by a certain underground railway company, to erect ventilators—hideous structures—on the Thames Embankment and at Westminster. It was only when the abominable inventions had begun to disfigure the metropolis that the discovery was made of the authorisation by a Private Parliament Bill. A bitter fight ensued in the Press and in Parliament against the ventilators, which only ended, after all, in a compromise. The Private Bill might have endowed the company with the right to stick their chimneys up in Westminster Abbey, or, as a clever burlesque writer pointed out at the time, to make a carriage road through St. Paul's. It was this very demon, the Private Bill, that Mr. Reade tilted at and overcame in the defence of his house, 19, Albert Gate, Knightsbridge. A party of speculative builders tried to capture the property. When they failed a certain peer "went for it" in a Private Bill, which provided for the extinction of seven of the houses, for the purpose of a new public road into the park. Mr. Reade, in his letters to the Press, demolished "the oligarch's plot," and warned Parliament and the public against Private Bills. This was some years ago, and yet it has been possible for a railway company to smuggle through Parliament a Private Bill giving them the right to destroy the beauty and usefulness of the Thames Embankment, and to pour out its underground smoke into the atmosphere near Westminster Abbey and the Houses of Parliament. It is interesting, just now, to quote Mr. Reade on this subject:—" When Private Bills come on," he says, " there is nobody in the House but the personal friends of the projectors. A job of this kind slides from a Bill into an Act in less time than it would take to hatch a serpent, and the House becomes the cat's-paw of a tyranny quite foreign to its own heart and principles. This is where the shoe really pinches. Only a few members have time or inclination to attend to these cursed Private Bills, especially when they are up to the neck in the Hellespont—and who can blame them?—and so a very little varnish carries them through. John Milton says very truly that even wisdom has its blind side. The times are high-minded, and the high-minded are unsuspicious; and so at Wisdom's gate Suspicion sleeps and thinks no ill where no ill seems."

III.

This volume of " Readiana" is full of excellent material for an estimation of the character of Charles Reade. His catholicity of feeling, his hatred of cant, his high sense of justice, his love for the suffering and the poor, are shown from first to last in his writings as well as in his life. What would have struck you next if you had known him well was the difference between Mr. Reade at home and Mr. Reade in print. Call upon him. He would receive you with the gentleness of a saint (not that I pretend ever to have known a saint, but you will appreciate the simile), talk to you with singular modesty, listen to you with the greatest respect, ask you to dinner, or to take a cup of tea, as one who receives a favour by your acceptance, and you would have gone away thinking of him as the mildest, sweetest, most long-suffering gentleman you ever met. But give him a grievance, tamper with his rights, tread on his moral corns, then put a pen in his hand, and you would find him a "slinger" of thoughts that breathe, of words that burn indeed. Not, my friends, that I ever experienced his wrath. On the contrary, he had always kind and sympathetic words for me. He took me by the hand, and said the first kind things to me when I came to London, over twenty years ago.

IV.

"Naboth's Vineyard" knows him no more, but 19, Albert Gate will always have an interest for his admirers, as the house in which nearly all his best works were written, and where he spent the happiest days of his life. He left there to live and die at 3, Bloomfield Villas, on the Uxbridge Road, in a comparatively new house, in a neighbourhood as different from the *rus in urbe* of Knightsbridge, "the only break in the hideous monotony of mediocrity," as it is possible to imagine. You get to it through cheap streets and busy thoroughfares, over tramways and under railway bridges. It is pleasant enough when you reach your destination, and the house has a southern frontage. Said the host, when I saw him last there, "Always select your abode so that your windows look out upon the south."

v.

Tall, well-built (once he must have been very powerful of limb), Mr. Reade had a singularly benevolent expression of face, bright grey eyes, a beard and moustache nearly white; he stooped slightly, and had a large, frank hand. Born in 1814, he was educated at Magdalen College, Oxford, graduated B.A. in 1835, was called to the Bar in the year 1843, and like some other great and famous men, discarded the law for literature. "Peg Woffington" was published in 1852. This was his first book. "And I got five pounds for it," he said to me twenty years ago, when I told him I had only received thirty-five on account, with prospective advantages, for my first; "be comforted, therefore; I was satisfied to get anything and be published." It is the old story of small beginnings, only that Charles Reade exhibited as high a capacity in his first as in his latest work. The freshness and beauty of "Christie Johnston" are not excelled even in "The Cloister and the Hearth," nor is there in the entire range of fiction any book written with a purpose designed to expose and reform some public evil which holds the reader with more mental grip as "Hard Cash" and "Put Yourself in His Place."

VI.

Among the most sincere mourners of Charles Reade was the late Wilkie Collins. The other day, chatting with a New York friend, he showed me a letter in which Collins paid a noble tribute to the generous and lovable character of Reade. Wilkie Collins for many years lived in York Place. You pass the house when going along Baker Street, as you drive to St. John's Wood to see a cricket match at Lord's. A solid, substantial English home, with a host who was always courtly and hospitable. He took delight in his work and would talk with you about it. Mr. Blackmore (the author of "Lorna Doone"), one of the most remarkable novelists of these days, dislikes, they say, to talk about his work. Neither will he give you his portrait for your wife's album. It is always your wife's, your daughter's, or your sister's album, for which you are collecting. Mr. Blackmore is literally a trader, a market gardener, not by necessity, but by choice. He has a beautiful place not far from a picturesque point of the Upper Thames, and

A BIT OF THE BLACKMORE GARDEN.

he sends fruit to the London market. The author of
"Lorna Doone," not by any means insensible to the

fame of that beautiful story, still prefers to discuss gardening rather than literature. If you try to introduce the subject of books you will find him drifting into horticulture, or raising points of natural history that would have gone home to the heart and fancy of Alphonse Karr, whose "Tour Round my Garden" offers to the young student a rare and dainty initiation into the mysteries of nature.

"I tried to talk of other novelists," said a friend of mine, fresh from a visit to Blackmore, "and he spoke of the ravages of the slugs among his strawberries, and he told me how he dealt with the marauding blackbird among his cherries." I believe Mr. Blackmore has never been photographed, nor will he sit for the purpose; in that respect he is like the late George Eliot, and it is only quite recently that Sir Edwin Arnold has consented to face the camera.

VII.

On the other hand, poor Wilkie Collins's features are familiar to the public—the short body, the large, powerful head. If you had seen him sitting at a table you might have thought him a giant; and when he rose you found he was not even of medium height. In this he resembled the late Douglas Jerrold. As the editor of a magazine, I once called upon Mr. Collins with proposals for a new story. He showed me with pride his latest novel printed in several foreign languages. I remember that it did me good to find a man who had made his mark so perfectly frank in showing me that his success gave him real pleasure. He spoke enthusiastically of the hopes he entertained of the book upon which he was then engaged. He told me that he was dramatising "The Moonstone." I ventured to hope that he would make much of the three dusky guardians of the stolen gem. In the novel they exercised an immense influence, full

of dramatic suggestiveness. "No," he said; "I have cut them out; I am afraid they would look like three negro minstrels on the stage." Mr. Collins in early life was on the literary staff of the *Leader*, one of the brightest and most brilliant of our weekly journals about five-and-thirty years ago. His first novel was "Antonina," which was bought and published by the elder Bentley. About three years afterwards (the interval being filled with several stories, including "Basil") he began to write for

Dickens in *Household Words*, since which time he has given to the world a series of novels that have thrilled the imaginations of millions of readers in all parts of the world, and added to the picture galleries of fiction such well-known creations as Count Fosco, Captain Wragge, and Geoffrey Delamayne.

VIII.

There has recently been some discussion concerning the merits of "The New School of Fiction," as represented by Messrs. Howells and James, and the foremost English writers. An attempt would seem to be afoot to disparage certain novelists on this side of the Atlantic, in order to strengthen the reputation of the newcomers. Posterity will put all this straight. Reade's position in fiction is not settled; and his American contemporaries are assuredly not yet "out of the wood." Apart from the admiration one feels for the authors of "A Chance Acquaintance" and "Daisy Miller," it seems too early for controversy as to the merits of the so-called new school, and that of Thackeray, Dickens, and Reade. The topic recalls to me a reminiscence of one of poor Henry Byron's comedies, that seems to fit the situation like the tag of a play. There is no harm in it, and the point lies between a play upon words and an expression of opinion. Two rival names are mentioned in it, both so good that the one complements the other, like the two harmonious colours on a painter's palette. The heroine of the comedy is a bright American girl, full of fun and patriotism. Praising her own country at the expense of the hero (her lover, by the way), she tells him that America has had to undertake even the task of teaching England how to spell, apropos of which she triumphantly demands: " What do you say to Webster ? " " Walker ! " responds the Englishman.

IX.

"AS YOU LIKE IT" AT POPE'S VILLA.

A Reminiscence of the Thames—Mrs. Langtry and Outdoor Plays—Under the Elms—A Lesson in Shakespeare—The First Rehearsal—Mrs. Labouchere and her Pupil—Personal Beauty—Can Acting be Taught.

POPE'S VILLA.

I.

THE American correspondent of the *Sunday Times* sends to that journal an account of Mrs. Langtry's Californian farm of 4500 acres, 1500 of which are planted with wheat. Mrs. Langtry is a rich woman. She made a fortune in about six years. Reading of her territorial purchases, her real estate, and her silver mine, all bought with the purse, not of Fortunatus, but of the successful actress-manager, I am reminded of my first formal introduction to her. It was on the eve of her first visit to America, and my description of the occasion is, I think, worthy of reconsideration, not only as a pleasant reminiscence, but as the forerunner of the outdoor plays given soon afterwards, no doubt on the hint conveyed in the Langtry incident, which not only attracted the attention of some next-door amateurs and professionals (Mr. Herman Vezin among the number), but was partly reprinted from my *New York Times* correspondence by the *Era*, in September 1882. I wrote this sketch on the 4th of the previous month. When the article reappeared in the *Era*, it was reported in London that the correspondent of the *New York Times* had been endowed with an annuity by Pope's Villa and Mrs. Langtry. But the journalist's chief delight in life is to be the fairy godfather at illustrious art cradles, and he is only too happy if his forecasts of good fortune are realised. Next to that are firstly, the delight of supplying his journal with the first of a good thing; secondly, to treat his pen to a new opportunity; and, thirdly, to earn the very large salary which his princely employers pay him. And that is how I came to chronicle the doings of a day at Pope's Villa, the leading points of which obtain a new interest to-day, on account of

Mrs. Langtry's remarkable success, and the formation of a company of " Pastoral Players."

II.

I have somewhere seen a picture of the garden scene of "The Decameron,' remote from the highway and " covered with trees and shrubs of an agreeable verdure." There was in the foreground a group of " lovely women and gallant men," dealing pleasantly with the " fleeting hour." I am reminded of that painting and wish I could convey to the reader a companion work in black and white. It is a scene on the Thames, a sunny summer afternoon, and to be truthful, I must say it is Sunday. High Church people in London allow a wide margin for Sunday recreation in the afternoon, if you begin the day by going to morning service. Some of the living figures in this garden picture on the Thames had been to church. Let me emphasise this fact in their moral and religious interest. A broad, velvety lawn, into the verdure of which your foot sinks at every step;

great elms and cedars that make deep shadows; beds of roses that respond to the sunshine in both colour

"AS YOU LIKE IT."

and perfume; a few garden seats in a retired corner; two ladies and two gentlemen sitting in the shade of elms and larches, and constituting an audience; one of the gentlemen, Mr. Henry Labouchere, Member of

Parliament. In presence of this audience, two ladies are reading and acting a scene from *As You Like It*, the performers being Mrs. Langtry and her friendly tutor, Mrs. Labouchere. The scene is in the garden of Pope's Villa (Mr. Labouchere's country residence), at Twickenham, the grounds of which are reached through the famous grotto constructed by the poet.

III.

There are few more delightfully situated houses on the Thames than the modern representation of Pope's Villa, with its lawns overhanging the river in front, and its quaint retreat of verdant grounds and gardens at the back. It was our humour on this summer afternoon to consider a certain green place, bounded by tall elms, a stage, the forest scene in *As You Like It*, and to have Mrs. Langtry and Mrs. Labouchere rehearse some passages of Shakespeare's comedy. I will venture to say the work was never more sweetly mounted, nor in more realistic fashion. The forest glade was idealised, it is true, in the well-rolled turf, the cultivated shrubs ; but the great trees that spread their branches overhead might well have stood foster brothers to the "greenwood" treasures of Amiens' song. Take note of this picture of a cultured ease, this realistic theatre, this ample stage, and well-contented audience ; no fees, no bustling entrance-hall, no noisy street, no cabs, no stuffy atmosphere, no "smoking strictly prohibited"; lounge chairs, cigarettes, a side-table with fruit and iced wine, and the actors in ordinary morning dress ; Mrs. Langtry in a pretty muslin delaine, with a sailor's hat ; Mrs. Labouchere in blue serge ; the one taking the *rôle* of Rosalind, the other that of Celia. This is the first rehearsal with an audience. The leading artist is slightly nervous—an excellent sign, and one which gives me hope of her ; for in the first days of her engagement at the Haymarket I thought her too self-conscious, and in a conversation with her on this Sunday at Pope's Villa, I found her fully sensible of the ordeal she had passed through.

"I have only understood the magnitude of what I undertook since the event has passed," she said. "Had I been so thoroughly aware of the difficulties that belong to a reasonably successful appearance on the stage as I am now, I would not have had sufficient courage to risk so great a venture. I was not nervous then ; I am now." "Which argues," I answered, "that you are making progress." "I really believe I am making way, and I hope to prove my gratitude for the kindness I have received by making myself worthy of the profession. Believe me, I never knew what real work was until now, nor what real happiness is. You know that in consequence of Mr. Langtry's losses in Ireland it has become, if not exactly necessary, at least very desirable that I should earn my own living.

I am doing that now, and more. I cannot tell you what intense pleasure it has given me to make a substantial present to my mother for the first time in my life. Some people think me a frivolous person, contented with dressing herself and being in society. They shall see. Since I resolved to become an actress, thanks to the wise advice and aid of Mrs. Labouchere, I have worked all the time—worked and studied without cessation—and during my provincial tour I have received such critical encouragement as induces me to hope for an ultimate success."

IV.

She looked her part. There was a tired expression about her eyes—those liquid eyes about which poets have sung, and which great painters have striven to realise on canvas. Study has given her face an intellectual expression, which adds somewhat of poetry to the pensiveness that is a notable characteristic of her beauty. There are possibly handsomer women than Mrs. Langtry, but none with greater charm of manner. Her features are singularly perfect, her eyes have "a languishing power of tenderness." It is not her fault if poets, painters, and society made her the belle of more than one London season, and it is a laudable ambition, surely, that permits her to seek approval for intellectual acquirements beyond those of personal beauty.

I may here remark that Mrs. Langtry has two qualifications for an actress—a fine appearance and a sympathetic voice. She speaks plainly, gives full value to her vowels, and does not under-estimate the importance of her consonants. Chatting with her over dinner, and after dinner on the lawn at Pope's Villa, I can quite understand the lady's success as a beautiful woman. You know what Addison says about the eye—" A beautiful eye makes silence eloquent; a kind eye makes contradiction an assent; an enraged eye makes beauty deformed. This little member gives life to every other part about us, and I believe the story of Argus implies no more than that the eye is in every part: that is to say, every other part would be mutilated were not its force represented more by the eye than by itself." Mrs. Langtry's eyes dominate her face and conversation. They adorn a natural grace of figure and movement, and lend eloquent interpretation to her words, which are spoken with a voice of singular sweetness.

V.

Let us now return to our opening picture. " Didst thou hear these verses?" asks Celia (Mrs. Labouchere). " O yes, I heard them all, and more too; for some of them had in them more feet than the verses would bear," and so on. Celia reads her part from the prompter's book. Rosalind speaks hers, suiting the

7

action to the word, the word to the action. She laughs, frowns; is merry and anxious as the story goes on; and I find in both elocution and action much to praise—the result of good tuition, and also of intelligent thoughtfulness on the part of the pupil. Mr. Labouchere, the reputed cynic, proves an excellent auditor; and I cannot help thinking to myself how little the world knows of its public men, their recreations, and their habits and customs. Despite his club life, and his Parliamentary work, Mr. Labouchere is an eminently domestic man, is fond of his home, does most of his writing there, and most of his thinking; "only drinks wine," he tells me, "when he can't get good water;" actually likes cake and tea, listens well to the most ordinary talker, and is, generally, a man of amiable manners, by no means disputative, and an excellent host.

VI.

The rehearsal having gone on sufficiently to show the great advance Mrs. Langtry had made in her art, and to demonstrate the truth of Boucicault's maxim that acting can be taught, it is interrupted by callers, who have entered from their boats and gondolas by the front way, and hunted us up through Pope's underground grotto. The actors, laying aside their books, mix with the audience; the new arrivals are taken into the general confidence; and the picture to which I originally invited your attention is still sweet, and calm, and quiet, except that the figures in it are now in movement. Host and guests break up into groups; a diplomat and a military officer take Mr. Labouchere aside to talk: a well-known painter and a young art student sit down with Mrs. Langtry to discuss the prospects of her voyage to America, and to wish her luck; a matronly lady and her wealthy lord discuss fruit and gardening with the hostess; and in a short time we are gradually drifting to the river front, where the guests, one after another, return to the boats, and gradually disappear towards the picturesque town of Twickenham, and that old ferry which a modern ballad has made famous on both sides of the Atlantic.

X.

"BETWEEN THE ACTS."

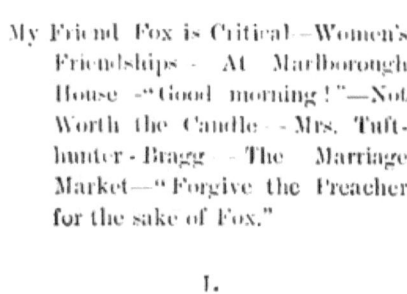
ROSALIND.

My Friend Fox is Critical—Women's Friendships—At Marlborough House—"Good morning!"—Not Worth the Candle—Mrs. Tufthunter - Bragg — The Marriage Market—"Forgive the Preacher for the sake of Fox."

I.

"Oh, yes," said Mr. Fox. "I like your unearthing that sketch of Mrs. Langtry's rehearsal of Rosalind: it was the beginning of the pastoral business; nobody said so, of course: Vezin wouldn't, why should he? A clever elocutionist, Vezin, and a good actor. Mrs. Labouchere broke with Mrs. Langtry, did she not, after all that Pope's Villa affection?"

"Yes, I have understood so."

"It couldn't be expected that so much mutual admiration could last between two women, eh?"

"Why not? Mrs. Labouchere made great sacrifices of time and convenience in the interest of her friend."

Fox is rather cynical, as you are aware, and I have often noticed that the better the cigar I give him, the more misanthropical he becomes. When he is unusually comfortable, in a physical sense, he seems to revel in comments and suggestions that are more or less unpleasant.

"There are no sincere friendships between women," he said, taking his cigar from his mouth to emphasise the remark with that snap, which, if you remember, we agreed was canine, not to say foxy.

"I don't agree with you," I replied.

"You wouldn't, of course; neither Mrs. Labouchere nor Mrs. Langtry were to blame. I have heard both their stories. But as you said the other day, art is a hard road to travel, and Mrs. Langtry looked further ahead than her theatrical sponsor."

"Well, let us be content, Fox," I said, "since they are; Mrs. Langtry has made both fame and fortune apart from her theatrical directress, and Mrs. Labouchere is a leader in Society and happy in her pleasant home-life. And the beginning of their artistic labours in the garden at Pope's Villa is none the less notable that the partnership so soon came to an end."

II.

"That may be so," Fox replied.

"May? may, it is," I answered. "The beginnings of things are always worth studying; they are always interesting, though to the careless eye they often seem insignificant; that tiny spring in Gloucestershire, which is the source of the Thames, for instance."

"And 'Gasaris,' with his £3 15s. in his pocket," rejoined Fox. "It is the same in regard to crime as art, the same in the matter of prigging and prosperity, it all begins low down. But what is prigging now-a-days? That's the question. Ask them up in the city and they can tell you; they ought to know. Scotland Yard gets very much puzzled over the question; but we shall know some day, when we have to interview St. Peter, eh? I wonder if we shall all stand in a row as they did at the Marlborough House Garden Party the other day: it seemed very odd to me. There were Mr. Gladstone, the Archbishop of Canterbury, Lord Salisbury, and no end of great men and good, all with their hats off, and in a semi-circle round the Queen, who, with the Lord Chamberlain at her elbow, selected the person she would like to speak with, and when she had done so sent the Lord Chamberlain to bring him to her. Very charming, no doubt, for those who were chosen; but for the rest—well, I was not exactly in the ring, but if I had been I shouldn't have liked to be passed over."

III.

"No, you wouldn't, Fox, and if you had been called up I dare say you would have gone down upon your knees, and waited for her Majesty to find a sword."

"No, sir," Fox replied with a snap, almost a bark, "I am not a tufthunter, a money-bag, nor a wind-bag; I am not a time-serving politician, and there is no sword of that kind for me; I don't expect it and don't desire it."

"There was a fox once in a fable who said something similar about certain fruit he professed he did not want," I replied, passing the bottle, and with my blandest smile.

"Good evening!" said my guest, and before I could apologise he was gone; but I knew that he had an engagement, and that the hour of the appointment was up; and Fox really has a regard for me that is not to be broken down by a jest, or even by an insult—if I were capable of insulting so old and valued a friend.

"Good morning," I called after him, "is the popular question, and it refers to soap."

He heard me. Pausing to look back through the half-closed door, he said: "Yes, I have used it, and Brown's soap is the best—good evening!"

Thus with a leading question you may often bounce the most fastidious and clever man into a frivolous response.

IV.

A curious fellow, Fox—gentleman, diplomat, detective. In France he would have been a power next the President; in Russia the friend of the Czar; in London he is on more or less familiar terms with princes, and I don't suppose Mrs. Tufthunter-Bragg or Mrs. Brixton-Bayswater would believe him if he told them that getting into Society is not worth the candle, and that the greatest snobs in Society (when they are there) are themselves. It is very curious to watch the wriggling of these ladies, especially when followed by half-a-dozen daughters who might be happy with their Bayswater or Brixton lovers, but whose mothers have "other views, my dear"; the other views being vaguely set upon one or more of the vapid youths who try to sing Arthur Roberts's songs, and smoke the same brand of cigars as that supplied to H.R.H. The marriage question is, no doubt, a serious business to materfamilias who has a number of daughters on hand, but the happy solution of it is not advanced by instilling into the girlish minds the idea that young women are a kind

MR. FOX.

of marketable commodity, and that their wanderings through what mamma calls Society are in the nature of a parade of their charms. Fox says he is glad he never married. A man with a family of girls is greatly to be pitied, he thinks; but Fox, moving about between

IN SOCIETY.

Kensington and Mayfair, and having special privileges of a social character, sees very much of one side of the marriage market. He does not see much of the father who regards local esteem as more conducive to happiness than general reputation, nor of the mother who believes in making home the happiest place on earth, nor of the daughters who have been brought up in this faith, and who have been taught to despise the meannesses that belong to the domestic economy of Mrs. Brixton-Bayswater and Mrs. Tufthunter-Bragg. Just as there is a vast amount of misery that is unknown to the world, so there is a vast amount of quiet happiness that is equally unproclaimed on the housetops. And depend upon it they are not the happiest people whose names you see most frequently in the Society papers. If you could only hear their querulous complaints at home, their petty criticisms of their neighbours, and become acquainted with the economical miseries of their efforts at keeping up appearances! For your sake I am glad you cannot. And when you hear people say unkind things of others, who are more prosperous than they, or who fail to find pleasure even in the successes of their friends, remember that so small a portion of enjoyment falls to most men and women that they cannot possibly feel much delight in the pleasure of others. The really and truly happy cannot be envious; therefore one ought to pity those who say unkind things of others, or who envy their neighbour's ox, his ass, or anything that is his.

I did not intend this present chat to drift into a sermon. Forgive the preacher for the sake of Fox; he began it. We will try a new bundle of cigarettes without him.

XI.

A CHAT WITH A PUBLISHER.

The Story of a Book—Ouida "First"—In a Popular Publisher's Room From a Window in Piccadilly—Ouida and the Proprieties—"Little Wooden Shoes" and "A Dog of Flanders."

I.

"PERSONAL conversations with the right men make interesting and reliable history," I said; "and what can be more entertaining than a talk with an eminent publisher about the authors whose works he exploits, and the joint results of their labours; for while an author has sometimes made a publisher, a publisher has sometimes made an author."

"If you think I can tell you anything that will interest your public," said Mr. Andrew Chatto, of the firm of Chatto & Windus, "you may certainly command me. An author yourself, I can rely on your discretion, and there is something new in the idea of a novelist interviewing a publisher—the lion and the lamb, you know!"

"Which is the lion and which the lamb? But we will leave that to the reader. In the first place, I have heard that there is a good trade story behind the publication of Mr. Justin McCarthy's 'History of Our Own Times.' Will you tell me what it is?"

"Yes," he replied. "Mr. McCarthy conceived the idea of writing a book entitled 'The Victorian Era,' which was to be an historical narrative. Introduced to a well-known firm of publishers, he entered into an arrangement to sell them the work for six hundred pounds. After a little while the publishers, learning that Mr. McCarthy was a Home Ruler, if not a Parnellite—they did not even know, it appears, that he was an Irishman—asked to be allowed to withdraw from the contract. Mr. McCarthy, who was greatly annoyed at the suggestion that he might mutilate history to suit his own private or political views, demanded compensation, and the publishers referred the settlement to the friend who had introduced the author to them. Then Mr. McCarthy came to me, and I at once agreed to publish the work for him on a basis of mutual profits. I suggested, however, that instead of 'The Victorian Era,' he should call the book 'The History of Our Own Times.' In the interval the other publishers reconsidered the situation, and asked to be allowed to revive the lapsed contract. It was too late. The work was in my hands, which, as it turned out, was a good thing for the author as well as for me. I have paid Mr. McCarthy up to the present time over five thousand pounds on account of his profits on 'The History of Our Own Times.'"

II.

Chatto & Windus are "Ouida's" publishers; they hold Charles Reade's copyrights; their names are on Swinburne's poems, and they are the English publishers of Artemus Ward, Mark Twain, Bret Harte, Julian Hawthorne, and other American writers. Chatto's father wrote the standard work on wood engraving which was published by Bohn.

"It was while trying to buy back from Bohn this copyright," said Chatto, "that led to my purchase of Bohn's library copyrights for twenty thousand pounds, most of which I afterwards resold."

"How did you come into the publishing business?"

"I was the assistant of J. C. Hotten, whose business I and Windus purchased from his widow for twenty-five thousand pounds, and we are really the successors of Hotten, though we do not adhere to the policy of our predecessor. For instance, he believed that the best way to force on an international copyright with America was to plunder American authors. We do not. An American author can secure a copyright in England by publishing here first. By that means Bret Harte, Mark Twain, and others enjoy all the privileges of this market as well as their own. We have paid Mark Twain over five thousand pounds for royalties on his books."*

III.

The scene of our conversation is eminently characteristic of London, and of the gentleman with whom I am talking. It is a room at the very top of the business premises of the firm, near the Circus end of Piccadilly. On the landing entrance is a large telescope (Chatto's recreation is science), in the doorway a fine St. Bernard dog, which rises to examine every visitor in these privileged regions. It is a large square room, the walls covered with original drawings of engravings, most of which have appeared in *Belgravia*, the centre of the room occupied by a large square table, upon which a frugal luncheon is laid (our meeting is at two in the day), and as you sit down before a well-cooked English chop and a bottle of Burgundy, you look upon a picturesque " roofscape "—a world of roofs

---

* American critics have pointed out that the International Copyright Act secures no new advantage in England. It will be seen by Mr. Chatto's remarks, made long prior to the New Act, that our American friends needed no protection on this side; they already enjoyed the privileges of copyright in Great Britain.

AT THE CIRCUS.

and chimney pots, the sky line broken up as artistically as the eye can desire. If you go to the window and look down, there below you is Piccadilly, busy with a multifarious traffic, the noise of which does not reach you high up among the many-shaped roofs, tiles, and smoke-stacks of the West End. Where the walls of the room are not wholly occupied with pictures there are well-filled bookcases. Over the mantelpiece are portraits of Mary Anderson and other public favourites. A piano and a microscope represent music and science—one stands near the door, the other near the window—so that the arts, science, trade, and social life have all a pleasant showing in the snuggery of these Piccadilly publishing offices. Do not imagine Mr. Chatto lives here. He has his country house, of course, his garden, his lawn, and his pastoral Sundays away from the turmoil of the metropolis. A genial, "cheery" fellow—dark, medium height, middle-aged, hazel eyes, and a countenance that is tell-tale to its owner's disposition—Mr. Andrew Chatto is a man whom an author might trust, I should say. He is certainly singularly sympathetic for a publisher, believes in his authors, likes to talk of them, was quite on intimate terms with Reade, and is so with Swinburne, and quite recently he paid a visit to Ouida at Florence.

"Tell me something one may print about Ouida."

"Well," he said, "some people have an idea that Ouida—Madame de la Ramé—is not an observer of what are called the proprieties of life. But she is, and a strict observer. A personal friend of the Queen

MADAME DE LA RAMÉ ("OUIDA").

of Italy, she prides herself on her blue blood. She is the daughter of an Italian aristocrat—one of the old noblesse—by an English mother, belonging to an old Gloucestershire family."

"Is that so?"

"Yes. She lives with her mother at Florence, where I visited her not long since."

"When does she write?" I asked.

"In the early morning. She gets up at five o'clock, and before she begins, works herself up into a sort of literary trance. She is very enthusiastic about her work."

"She refuses, as a rule, to have her stories published in serial form?"

"A DOG OF FLANDERS."

"Yes; she does not consider it artistic. Serial form, I suspect, does not suit her method, nor the construction of her novels. Her early works were published by Tinsley and by Chapman & Hall. Our first business with her was in the publication of 'Friendship.'"

"What is her most popular novel?"

"'Under Two Flags,'" he replied, "and I think it is her best."

"What about 'Moths'?"

"Not so great a sale as 'Under Two Flags.'"

"It is a pity," I could not help remarking, "that a woman who could write 'Little Wooden Shoes,' and 'A Dog of Flanders,' should have perpetrated that libel on English Society entitled 'Moths.' I don't ask your opinion on that point."

"There is nothing more pure or more beautiful in fiction than two of the stories you have mentioned," he replied, handing me his cigar-case; and while I light one of his choice Habanas, I will ask you to let me make it an excuse for concluding this chat with a publisher "in our next."

XII.

CRITICS CRITICISED.

The Publisher and the Press—Library Readers of Fiction—The Potentiality of the Novel—Author and Publisher—An Honest Sentiment.

I.

CHARLES READE.
From a Sketch taken thirty years ago.

"Which of Mr. Charles Reade's books sell best?" I asked my friend, Mr. Chatto, the publisher.

"'Hard Cash' and 'Never Too Late to Mend.' The public think these are his best novels, so do I. The Press differ from this judgment. The critics give the palm to 'The Cloister and the Hearth.' But it is certainly not as masterly nor so artistic as the other two; it is overcrowded with incident."

"What are your views about the influence of criticism in these days?"

"Criticism, to be of any real value, should be signed," he said; "we might then expect to get honest, reliable, authoritative criticism. As it is, criticism is too often relegated to inexperienced writers, and they frequently sit in judgment upon volumes they do not understand. My experience is that some of the best books receive the worst notices in the Press, and some of the worst books get the best notices. I do not desire to run down the influence of the Press; it would be absurd to attempt to do so, and especially in a publisher; but I must say that I think the success of a book is made very much in the same way as a play: people read a book, like it, talk of it, recommend it, just as people talk of a piece at the theatre; criticism, properly handled, and by responsible writers, would be of great service, no doubt."

"The work of criticism is arduous, and not very satisfactory to those engaged in it—don't you think so?—especially considering the rubbish that is published in the shape of books?"

"Yes, I quite agree with you there; and that reminds me to say a word for the library system of publishing books that obtains in England—a distinct thing from all American systems of publishing. There is one three-volume novel published every day in the year, and one-half of these works are paid for by the authors—they never pay their expenses—and not one-tenth of the entire lot is ever reprinted. Now, the library system is a sort of sieve, through which this quantity of fiction is poured, and thus the chances of discovering a good novel are multiplied. The library readers are the tasters, then come the critics, and between the two the bad novels, as a rule, should disappear, and the good ones remain, like the ore in a gold-washer's cradle."

II.

"What class of literature has most readers?"

"Fiction," he replied. "Oh, yes, fiction—the potentialities of fiction are developing enormously."

"The taste of the moment," I asked, "is it not rather in favour of what may be called psychological studies, sceptical essays, and semi-religious discourses, descriptions of travel and scenery, with a thin thread of story holding them together—novels of character rather than novels of plot and dramatic construction?"

"Yes, and you say well when you speak of the taste of the moment, for it will change. Now, to my mind Charles Reade is the greatest novelist of the age. The public to-day do not think so, but the next generation will, and, depend upon it, the taste for mere light, sketchy story-telling, without strength of plot and incident, and strong, firmly-drawn character, will go out, and is going out."

"James Payn's books have a large sale? And Besant and Rice's?"

"Yes, we publish both."

MR. WALTER BESANT AND THE LATE MR. JAMES RICE.

"People often ask curious questions about the collaboration of Rice and Besant. It is not fair to go behind the work of such clever novelists and reveal the system, eh? What do you think?"

"Hardly," he replied; "but this much may be said, that Rice was not what you call the literary partner in that combination. He was the practical man in the way of construction, and his suggestions may be traced in some of the humorous passages of their work. He was a very pleasant, conscientious, good fellow, Rice, an excellent journalist, for many years London correspondent of the *Toronto Globe*. What I think essential in a novelist is a thorough belief in his story and in his characters. Now I was once in Edinburgh with Charles Reade; we went up to Arthur's Seat. 'There,' said Reade, pointing far away in the distance, 'that's where Christie Johnston caught the herrings.' He regarded it, you see, as history, the incident an accomplished fact, the woman a reality!"

III.

"You have told me something about your success, now about your failures. What about your young writers?"

"I have no failures," he answered laughing—and Chatto can laugh heartily—"my friends tell me all my geese are swans, but I tell them no, they are only ducklings that grow into swans."

"Christie Murray, the author of 'Joseph's Coat,' was an ugly duckling?"

"Yes, he is now a swan," he replied; "I think his

'Joseph's Coat' may fairly take rank among the best examples of modern fiction."

"It is pleasant to hear a publisher speak appreciatively of the authors with whom he is associated. There are publishers, I believe, who know little or nothing of the books they introduce to the world."

"You see," he replied, "I am my own reader; I read several novels each week. I rely on my own judgment; I don't leave the duty of saying what manuscript is good or bad to others. I undertake all that. And it is no child's play, as you will admit, when I tell you that we have published over four hundred different works of fiction, and own nearly all the copyrights of them. And apart from the profit of the work, I rejoice as much, I think, as the author himself when one of the books we publish makes a special hit. You remember the 'agent in advance' described in Charles Reade's 'Woman Hater'? Well, I think a publisher should be as devoted to an author as that agent was to his employer. Men who do not read the books they undertake to publish are no better than mere tradesmen."

"An honest sentiment," I said, "and one for which all authors should honour you."

"I am glad to hear an author say so," he replied, and so we parted; Mr. Chatto to take up the thread of his day's business in the counting-house, I to stroll homeward and write this sketch. A stout policeman

"ON DUTY."

conducting a crowd through the congested traffic of Piccadilly Circus took me in with the rest; I walked along Regent Street to Regent's Park. The weather was warm and sunny. Thousands of people were out taking advantage of the first glimpse of summer. Regent's Park was crowded with cricketers, a military band was playing a selection from *Faust*, the elephants were trumpeting a concert on their own account in the Zoo, long lines of carriages were waiting near the North Gate to set down and take up the guests at an artist's "At Home," the grass was green, the trees "bounfiful of umbrageons leaf," and I came to the conclusion for the thousandth time that London is a delightful city.

XIII.

THE SALVATION ARMY.

A Remarkable Organisation—Fanatic or Philanthropist?—Revivalism—Dinah Morris and Circe—Refuges for the Lost.

I.

GENERAL BOOTH.

THE Salvation Army is a very remarkable organisation. It has done good. It may have done harm. It may be a curse, it may be a blessing. How much it is one, or how much the other, is problematical. Whether the founder of it is a fanatic or a philanthropist I cannot say. He is, at all events, a clever administrator. His policy is one of novelty, of mystery. He likes to startle the public. "Be odd," is the essence of his instructions to his active disciples. "Be peculiar religiously; let everything about you show that the forces you represent will introduce some novelty when they come." These are, I understand, the founder's own words, comprising part of his instructions to his followers, and they act upon his orders with military preciseness. They are "peculiar," but whether they are "peculiar religiously" is an open question. On the march they have various bands of instrumentalists; sometimes it is a brass band with a predominance of drum; sometimes it is a band of guitars and tambourines; sometimes it is a vocal band with accordion accompaniments. There is always a leader who walks first, a sort of drum-major who shouts and beats time. He walks backward, in which exercise he must have had great practise, his efficiency being perfect. The captains and commanders are very much in earnest; so are rogues; so are thieves; these captains and commanders may, however, be true religionists. They have a peculiar physiognomy; they have hatchet faces, pale complexions, thin lips, wiry frames, and a tendency to jump. "The labourer is worthy of his hire." They are paid for their services and they work hard. Some of them preach or narrate their religious experiences. Their supreme commander does not encourage "sermons." He is in favour of narratives, anecdotes, and humour. This being known, the "preachers" vie with each other in a certain hilarious profanity. They indulge in a mirthful familiarity with holy names, and express a fearless intimacy with the personality and wishes of God and Christ. But their

strong point is music. The English people may
not be great musicians, but they like to sing and
they love to march to martial strains. The Salvation Army gives them popular tunes, variety-show
melodies, Moody and Sankey hymns, and aggressive
words to aggressive measures. These vocal and
instrumental recreations are pleasing to the ignorant
and the emotional. They march and shout and sing
and are comfortable. The founder and supreme head
boasts that he has discovered a happy religion. And
so he has. The self-righteous, the ignorant, the
singers and shouters, the men who like military
uniforms and can get a bit of cheap and harmless
soldiering out of the organisation, are happy; anything is a relief from their monotonous round of
drudgery. The churches are very dull and prosaic.
The church-goers supplicate the Throne of Grace.
The Salvationists go for it, attack it, bombard it,
assault it, take Peter by storm, seize his keys, open
the gates, and march into Paradise with triumphant
anthems, with "timbrels and with shawms," with
dancing and with songs.

II.

It is another phase of revivalism. It is well known
in America, where they have it in vast camp-meetings,
in tent missions, in anti-rum organisations, in Shaker
societies, in free-love excitements, in Mormonism. It

is all in one direction—religious mania. Many honest people are engaged in it, weak, kindly men and women; and the results may be good or bad. It is difficult in these days, or in any days, to say how much good or how much harm so-called "religious" demonstrations do. But one cannot fail to notice that the wire-pullers always seem to have a good time. Mr. Booth (I beg his pardon—"General" Booth), the head and front, the founder, manager, treasurer, and everything of the Salvation Army, is said to be a rich man—rich, I presume, in heavenly blessings, as well as rich in worldly wealth. He began the business poor. He has all his family in it. They are a power in the state. They govern the army. It is *their* army. They receive the subscriptions. They own the halls and chapels and paraphernalia; and they render an account to their "heavenly Father," who is, I have no doubt, fully represented by an earthly auditor.

III.

> Fire away, fire away,
> Fire away, fire away,
> With the Gospel gun we'll fire away,
> Mighty victories have been won
> With the great salvation gun,
> Stand your ground and fire away!

These lines are the refrain of one of General Booth's favourite hymns. They represent his policy of persistence and push. He is a great man to-day, General Booth. He looks like a Hebrew. He has a big, hooked nose, but he is as true-born a Christian as the most snub-nosed of his officers. A tall, long-haired, hooked-nosed, bright-eyed, thick-lipped, goatee-bearded

"DINAH MORRIS" AT WHITBY.

gentleman, in a military uniform, he is a picture of splendid audacity. His wife was a factor in the work —ought I to say factoress? She was a pleasant-looking lady, in a simple Quakerish dress, a comely, plump, amiable woman, and kindly at heart, I feel assured. She preached and sang in comforting contrast to the fiery energy of her husband.

IV.

In country places the Salvationists recruit into their ranks many good and earnest young people, who are anxious to be useful to the world and to advance the work of Christ. They are church members, Sunday-school teachers, with naturally pious instincts. Not long since, at Whitby, in Yorkshire, I saw the beginning of the local organisation. The head of it was a girl of twenty-five. She recalled to my mind Dinah Morris, in "Adam Bede," and she preached in a sweet and tender way, and to the singing on the march played a tambourine. This latter exercise was unlike George Eliot's heroine, but in this instance it seemed quite correct. She was dressed in black, with a neat straw bonnet. She wore a small linen collar and white linen cuffs. Her dress fell gracefully about her figure. Neither crinoline, crinolette, nor "dress improver" interfered with the natural swing of her gait. Her face was pale, her eyes soft and large, and she had a melodious voice. She was the sort of creature Joan of Arc might have been. Half a dozen women similarly attired, eight or nine fishermen, and a dozen boys and artisans followed her, singing a Moody and Sankey hymn. She led them, beating time on her tambourine and singing, now walking backward, now forward, always graceful and picturesque, whatever she did. Now, if General Booth would send such a woman as that into the dens of London infamy, to induce her fallen sisters to lead a good life, he might hope for converts: but some time ago four of his female

SALVATION LASSES ON SUNDAY MORNINGS

soldiers, two of them with guitars, were chaffed and hustled at midnight in the Haymarket by a crowd of "fast" men and women; and what could they expect? It requires a special "call," a veritable Dinah Morris, to face Circe on her own threshold; and there is a time for this, as for all things, and the time is not midnight, but in quieter hours, when the sun shines, when the finery of the streets is laid aside, when the influence of the champagne has fizzed out, with a headache and a touch of remorse to follow. But General Booth is a sensationalist; he likes a row, a police case, a newspaper protest; so in the height of "The Maiden Tribute" business he sent his army girls into the streets where fast men and women most do congregate—sent them with guitars to rescue the victims of Circe. They were told to go home; Circe's lady disciples and "worshippers of Venus" called them fools, and jeered at them. The next day a correspondent wrote to his evening paper to complain of the conduct of the police on the occasion. Then another correspondent wrote to defend the police. Upon this out comes an appeal from Booth for £20,000, to be spent in refuges for the victims of the lust and cruelty of wicked men. I wonder if the money has come in. If such a sum were well spent, it would prove a useful lever for good. These kind of refuges have hitherto not proved very successful. Perhaps they are not well managed. That something of the kind is wanted everybody must admit. The subject is a more or less controversial one. My friend, Mr. Aaron Watson, has sent me his "Brown Studies," and he has something to say that is interesting about our Salvation friends. We will dedicate it to a separate bundle of cigarettes.

XIV.

HOW IT ORIGINATED.

Mr. Booth and His Recruits—The Army—The General Regulations
—"Chuckers Out"—Suggestions—What Fox Thinks about It—
"In Darkest England."

I.

THE Salvation Army, according to Mr. Aaron Watson, is the development of a Christian mission which was started, about 1879, in the East End of London. It was the work of Mr. Booth. He was a Nottingham man, born there in 1829. It has been claimed for him that he was a clergyman of the Church of England, but his origin was very humble. He was never an ordained servant of the Church; he was a minister of the Baptist New Connexion at Nottingham. His ardent and enterprising spirit was not satisfied with the provinces; London was his field. He became a travelling preacher—a stroller—holding forth anywhere, and living on true apostolic principles. He worked his way. There are always members of every Church to help their own propagators of the Gospel. Booth marched into the "Modern Babylon," started the London East End Mission, and converted it into the Salvation Army. On the 14th of May, 1882, he made his first big demonstration. He called a "Council of War" and a "Friendly Congress." He called it sensationally, he called it by proclamation, and made the day a red-letter one by inaugurating his Congress Hall at Lower Clapton, collecting for the Army work the sum of £7,000. His recruits came in from all parts of England, in uniforms marked with the letter "S," and with banners bearing the strange device of "Blood and Fire." Among the crowd was a company of women, known as the "Hallelujah Lasses"; and didn't they sing and beat their tambourines! There never was such a religious orgie. Among the men, a "converted sweep" and a "hallelujah giant" were conspicuous; and Booth led the music, and gave the occasion its "go" and "vim," while, at intervals, his quiet, gentle, eloquent wife calmed "the raging tempest of human passion" with pleasant words. But it was a terribly noisy day, and the noise has never ceased. It breaks in upon quiet seaside retreats; it is rampant in sober cities at their soberest sabbath hours; it takes possession of the parks; it howls, and sweats, and drums, and shrieks in every London suburb; it invades Switzerland and France; it has gone forth to India; it threatens the colonies; it has been heard in America; it is filling the world with its noisy din, and shutting out the sun with its flaring "blood and thunder" banners. Where will it end? And when?

II.

A few years since, General Booth chartered a steamer, and sent his "Life Guards" to Hull on a mission into Yorkshire. They had a band of forty pieces, were dressed in Life Guards' uniforms, with white Indian helmets. How far the Government is wise in permitting this burlesque of the troops it is hard to say. The General not only dresses his men in military attire, but he has a book of "Orders and Regulations," which is, by the way, a very clever and keen adaptation of the Army volume. It lays down rules for collecting money, for the hire of buildings, and generally for keeping up the funds and efficiency of the Army. There is one "dodge" of the General's which is strikingly characteristic. When he wants to make a special push for money at a big service or meeting he flies what he calls " canaries." These are yellow strips of paper, with a form of " I promise to pay," etc., printed upon them, and room for a signature and an address. The General rightly estimates the value of the proverbs, " Strike while the iron is hot," and " Make hay while the sun shines." Many persons at a religious meeting, or at public assemblages, under the influence of orators, and music, and crowds, would put exceptional sums into the collection-plate if they had them in their pocket-books. Booth supplies them with facilities to be generous ; he " flies his canaries," and they come back to him fluttering gaily among the gold and silver.

III.

The Salvation Army has had many physical as well as moral battles. It insisted upon marching in battalions along the Strand. This was one of its gravest mistakes. It lost its standards, and some of its members lost their liberty. There is so much real practical freedom in this country that those who deliberately break the laws deserve to be severely punished. General Booth does not, I believe, desire his troops to fly in the face of the law any more than he wishes them to fly in the face of Providence ; but he wishes them to make a noise in the world, to proclaim their mission, and even to run the risk of imprisonment rather than not do their utmost to preach the Gospel and bring sinners into camp. He also has wonderful arrangements to put sinners out of the camp. Among his troops are many tall, strong men; these are employed largely, to use the vernacular, as "chuckers out." I think I once narrowly escaped an encounter with a chucker out. "Come and be saved," or words to that effect, invited me into one of the Salvation camps. I entered. A giant, evidently a chucker out, barred my way. "I have come to be saved," I said. "It is too late," he replied. "Is it ever too late to be saved?" "Yes, sir," he said, emphatically. "But there is an unanswerable authority who says it is never too late." "It's ten o'clock," he replied; "you can't come in,

THE "CHUCKER OUT."

and that's all about it." He squared his shoulders at me threateningly, and after a little more talk, proposition and repartee, I decided that I would not do battle with the Salvation giant.

IV.

But I would suggest to the General that when he puts out invitations to come and be saved, he should at the same time fix the hours of business, or take a leaf out of a greater and an older organisation, and keep his doors always open to the sinner and the wayfarer of the street. I have on many occasions listened to the out-door harangues of the Army preachers; they have only one recommendation—their orations are very short, but as a rule they are not comforting; they are appeals to turn from the devil and flee; they are full of intimations that Christ is waiting for the audience then and there assembled; "waiting at the gate" is a favourite phrase; it is a gospel of cowardice, not of duty, not of worldly as well as heavenly happiness; it is a gospel of brimstone; it has no home comfort in it; no suggestion of the happiness of a quiet conscience; no account is taken of the delight that comes from the practice of kindness; it is a gospel of sound and fury; come and be saved from hell; don't come for love; come out of the way of the devil, who goes about like a roaring lion. I am

THE GENERAL

told that you must be teetotal to be a Salvationist; this is a strong argument in favour of the Army. It is a hard tax upon those districts where the civil troops meet every Sunday, with their drums and trumpets: could not some arrangements be made for varying the muster-grounds, and thus give the quarters now weekly assailed an occasional vacation?

The Army is by no means without its good and useful features, and a little concession in the case of complaints would do it no harm.

v.

Fox having strolled into my room and read the proofs of my notes on the Salvation Army, proffers the remark that he has no belief in the good results of the organisation. "Have you not noticed," he asks, "that there have been in the provinces several cases before the police, in which it was shown that the Army has been the moral retreat of thieves and wicked women?"

"No," I reply; "but one must not judge a body by individual backsliding: otherwise what about Scotland Yard?"

I am free to confess that when I want to push Fox into a tolerant frame of mind I hark back to the Scotland Yard scandal of a few years ago.

"There have been dishonest journalists, too," he answers, "as well as conspiring detectives."

"Of course, of course," I answer; "we are born in sin and shapen in iniquity, and that is the

Salvationist cry. I can imagine many cases of misery and darkness, of ignorance and criminal wretchedness, where the Salvationist preacher may

have brought comfort, and changed a life of gloom and hopelessness into one of resignation, if not content. It is

ON THE WAR-PATH.

a great thing if you can persuade some lonely wretch who has not a friend in the world that there is One above anxious to help and console him, and give him all his heart can desire in the next world."

"Ah," says Fox, "I see you have made up your mind to go in for the Army."

"Not I, i' faith; but I am willing to acknowledge the good there may be in it."

"When you can find it, eh? You speak of the pretty feminine scene at Whitby. That has captured your imagination, I fancy; but look at the 'joskins' who march about London."

"They do not appear to me to be 'joskins,'" I reply; "rather the opposite. What I fear about them is that some are designing fellows, in for notoriety and easy living, while others are simply fanatics."

"I do not refer to the leaders," says Fox, "but to the idle, open-mouthed recruits; the loafers of the streets; the stolid, ignorant residuum. And as for the leaders, I would like you to follow some of them home, and see how they live and what they do. Hypocrisy is a growing power in the land. As for General Booth—well, look at him; look at his mouth; if you don't believe that, look at his hands!"

"I don't want to look at either," I reply; "I believe he is doing good. It may not be the highest form of good; but if he only keeps half his Army out of the public-houses, and exercises a certain amount of moral discipline on the rest, I don't care how many 'joskins,' idlers, loafers, nor even thieves, he can recruit. The more the merrier!"

"Good evening," says Fox.

"Good evening," I naturally reply; but I decline to accept my friend's revision of this present after-dinner chat.

VI.

"Nothing succeeds like success." Newspapers in which, for years, Booth and his scheme were treated with contempt, are now his earnest supporters. Even as recently as "The Maiden Tribute" sensation, when it was supposed that the Army was at the back of Mr. Stead, the great journals would have nothing to do with him. To-day, under the inspiration of "In Darkest England," he has "fetched" the Press, and the Public, and Mr. Bancroft. A remarkable man, "General Booth." Heaven knows there is poverty and misery enough in the land. The Government being too busy with Timbuctoo and "the wrongs of Ireland," it is very good of General Booth to ask the public to give him a million to take over the duties of Parliament; and who shall say the stage is not moral and generous, when one of the first thousands on account of the said million comes out of a managerial pocket?

XV.

THE GOOD OLD DAYS.

A Novel Exhibition—The Norwich Coach and the Cheltenham Rival—"The Fly"—The first Mail Coaches—"Fox says the Coach is a Fraud nevertheless."

I.

DID you happen to see a unique Exhibition, *apropos* of coaching, that inaugurated the driving season of some ten years ago? There is no more nationally interesting story than that of coaching, and to-day it is a delightful pastime, in which the rich help their poorer fellow-subjects to enjoy the air. Coaching should have had some special recognition in the Jubilee year. Nero, Hector, and Nestor were coachmen, and since Horace immortalised a good charioteer, coaching has continually occupied the Anglo-Saxon mind. Captain

Malet says so, and he is not only an accepted authority, but it was he who took London by the button-hole and demonstrated the fact in that memorable exhibition. Wandering along Bond Street, looking for some pleasant picture gallery for half an hour's shelter from the rain which falls more or less during every day of our English spring, I halted opposite a unique announcement: "An Exhibition of Pictures, Illustrative of the Old Coaching Days." I entered and found that Captain Malet, of the 18th Hussars, had collected, borrowed, begged, and bought some hundred of pictures, models, and relics of coaching in Great Britain. I was not only in presence of "glorious reminiscences of the past" on the walls and under glass cases, but I suddenly made the acquaintance of a score of representative old men and women who were having a delightful time in reviving their memories of the age before railway trains with Captain Malet's pictures of "the good old days."

II.

Among the relics was the off hind panel of the original Brecon coach, several printed notices of days of running, guards' horns of 150 years ago, time-pieces fixed in bags, and some examples of old harness. But the chief interest of the show centred

in the pictures. They had been brought from all
parts of the land, and were enough to drive "a whip"
mad with delight. They were from the easels of such
artists as Henderson, Pollard, Aiken, and other
equally well-known painters of scenes on the road.
"The Hull, Lynn, and Lincoln Mail" is, perhaps,
Henderson's *chef d'œuvre*. It is a picture not to be
forgotten by any one of artistic perception, while to a
lover of coaching it is a delicious study. "At the
break of day the mails are seen meeting on the Great
North Road on their way up. In the centre of the
picture and on the box, holding the ribbons of the
Hull Mail, sits that great coaching artist and patron
of the road, the late Mr. George Alliston, who is
exchanging morning greetings with Harry Davis,
engaged in tooling the Lynn on his right. Coming
up behind, through the grey of the summer mist, is
seen the Lincoln, his off leader moped. The loading
of the coaches, the outside passengers half-asleep, and
shivering under the influence of the cold dews of
daybreak, are admirably told."

III.

While one feels a thrill of delight in contemplating
the old picturesque mode of travelling, an inward
prompting of gratitude to Mr. Pullman pays due
tribute to the luxury of steam locomotion. There is
a picture of "The Norwich Coach on the Road with

Turkeys at Christmas time," which would have appealed to the sentiments of the creator of old Weller.

> "It is a Christmas Coach, I vow,
> And whirls along with pride,
> For all its outside passengers
> Are food for the inside."

Thus sings the rhyming humorist of the time with this fine old picture in view. The same pen must have "celebrated" "The Norwich Coach," which is depicted by the same brush entering Bull Yard, Aldgate, groaning with Christmas cheer.

> "What a load!
> With bottles broach 'The Norfolk Coach,'
> As good a toast as heard is,
> And long live they who feast to-day
> Upon its Christmas turkeys."

"The Cheltenham Rival" is a stirring work by Henderson. It is said to be an excellent likeness of this well-known stage-coach, which was famous in its latter days for its splendid team of greys. It started daily from the Belle Sauvage Yard, Ludgate Hill, where the printing works of Cassell, Petter, and Galpin now stand. Sir Henry Peyton frequently drove, and always patronised this coach, the picture of which is said by Capt. Malet to be worthy the attention of coach-builders of the present day.

THE GOOD OLD DAYS. 147

IV.

Every phase of coaching was illustrated in this notable exhibition, showing the difficulties of the roads in all weathers and at all seasons, and from the

THE CHELTENHAM RIVAL.

earliest times. It was, in short, a pictorial history of the subject, and by the light of a " Map of the Grand Roads of England in 1679 " the pleasures and perils of charioteering may be thoroughly realised.

A coachman in King William's or Queen Anne's time had his hands pretty full, for the roads even in London were, Capt. Malet reminds us, full of pits and hollows. To get through a long street in wet weather without either sticking fast, breaking down, or being turned over by some reckless carman, was something to boast of in those days. The coach-box was then a box indeed, full of tools and materials for repairing damages, and the coachman was not infrequently as much an adept at tinkering as he was at driving. The box was covered with a hammer-cloth to hide the implements which were continually called into requisition. Capt. Malet says the best specimen of coach-building extant of this period is the Speaker's coach, to be seen at the Royal Mews. Three or four miles an hour was considered so good a pace at the latter end of the last century that the coach which averaged this speed earned for itself the characteristic title of "The Fly." The mail-coach, introduced for the first time in 1784, however, altered this state of things. The idea of the mail-coaches originated with Mr. Palmer, who took his notion from the stage-coaches. The mails and the stages rivalled each other in their smartness and turn-out; but the mails had a show day once a year, which lifted them upon higher ground than the stages could reach, and left their rivals humbly in the rear. On the Sovereign's birthday, each year, the whole of the mail-coaches (numbering fifty in 1836) paraded from the manufactory at Millbank to London, past St. James's Palace to the General Post Office and back again. The Royal Family always assembled in the palace to witness the procession.

V.

"For my own part," remarked Fox, who had somewhat cynically glanced at the proof of this scrap or two of after-dinner chat, "I think the coach an overrated vehicle so far as regards comfort ; picturesque, if you will, but a fraud as to seating capacity and a delusion as to speed."

"Indeed!" I said, somewhat taken aback at Fox's sweeping denunciation of the favourite mode of British locomotion.

"In the first place there is only one outside seat a fellow cares for, and that is the one next the driver. This is the seat *par excellence*, and even on that seat your legs are dangling about without footboard or rest, unless you choose to sit in a cramped attitude. Is not that so?"

"Well, it may be," I said, for I like to hear Fox talk, and he is easily intimidated, though you might not think so when you come to study his egotistical habit of thought and speech.

"What other seat on the outside do you care to occupy?"

"I prefer the box seat," I answer.

"My dear sir, there is no other seat; and what about the inside? Did any of Dickens's descriptions of the coach—and he was an enthusiast about it—make you hanker after the days before railroads?"

THE BOX SEAT.

"Yes," I replied, defiantly, "his descriptions of the halfway-houses, the jolly inns, and the genial landladies."

"Oh, yes," said Fox, "that is all very well; but I tell you the coach is picturesque, but not comfortable, and as for speed, were you ever in Moscow? Well, then, you should see the drosky, and even the omnibus go: up hill and down, it is all the same."

"But surely you don't tell me that the Russian omnibus is a fine vehicle?"

"No, horrible; but I am speaking of speed; it and the drosky, and, indeed, almost anything on wheels, must have beaten our coaches even in the palmy days of the Brighton platers."

"Nonsense," I remark.

"It is not nonsense, my dear sir; I tell you they go just the same, the Russian horses, up hill and down, no stopping, no pausing, a regular rush."

"And tumble," I venture to jerk in.

"No, sir, not a rush and tumble, a rush and go, a steady, tremendous scamper."

"But what about cruelty to the horse?"

"I don't say the horse is as well treated as ours; but at least his mane is not cropped, his tail is not shorn, and he is shod with some regard to comfort and usefulness."

"Ah, I am glad to hear that; there is nothing more painful in bad weather than to see the 'bus horses scratching their way up Ludgate Hill or slipping and sliding up from the bottom of Waterloo Place to Piccadilly Circus. The time will come, I hope, when horses will have a removable shoe, a shoe that can be taken off when he goes to his stable for rest and refreshment."

"Shake," said Fox, imitating an American friend of ours, and putting out his hand.

I shook, and Fox remarked that if I would add this bit of practical common-sense to the — well, to the rest of my chat — my "Cigarette Papers," for once in a way, would be worthy to follow the best dinner and the best dessert the best club could put upon its best table. Fox is both rude and cynical, and very well satisfied with himself; but I like him, nevertheless. There are some men whose pessimism is even more pleasant than the optimism of other men; some whose vanity is far less ostentatious than the modesty of others. I repeat, I like Fox—sometimes.

XVI.

MANY THOUGHTS ON MANY THINGS.

Don't be Successful—The Unappreciated—An Age of Gossip—Fox Intervenes—The Novel of the Future—A New Literary Era—Bateman and *Charles the First*—A Reminiscence of Cyfarthfa—At Supper with Irving—"To meet the Count, Countess, and Baron Magri"—The Trees at Bournemouth.

1.

If you would be happy don't be successful. Mediocrity that thinks itself great is perhaps the most desirable lot. Have a high opinion of yourself. If you don't get on, ascribe it to the envy, hatred, and malice of your opponents. Of course, they are numerous enough to handicap your efforts. They have influence; alas! you have only your genius If you are a pressman, and your brethren are continually occupied in obstructing your progress, you will find satisfaction, however obscure your medium of attack, in reviling the successful man who, no doubt, occupies the place you would be filling if your genius had its due recognition. It is all very well for Charles Dickens to have left it on record that he found no lions in his literary or journalistic path. He was a favourite of fortune and got his opportunity. Besides, George Cruikshank wrote several of his novels. The real happiness in life, no doubt, lies in not being successful. It gives you such a splendid position in your own estimation. And if you have a wife and children they will sympathise with you and fight your battles every day, after their scanty dinner, with heartfelt feeling, even if they encourage a secret suspicion that you are a fraud.

II.

I met our old friend Superbus the other day. He is not successful; but he edits a little sheet of curious gossip and opinion, which ought to sell by thousands and be quoted in *The Times*, but does not sell and is not quoted; and he falls foul of friends who have tried to help him, kindly brethren of the quill who have not had time to drift with him into the back slums of their craft, and, oh! how he "goes" for them! It would do you good to see how he slashes into one who gave him his first chance in journalism, encouraged his faltering muse, sat by his bed when

he was sick, and brought him medicinal aid at a
critical moment—absolutely, in fact, saved his life;
and to-day has, "for auld lang syne," only a gentle
friendly feeling for him. Not that the good Samaritan
himself is too successful; he is one of the hardest
workers in London; but he keeps clear of the back
streets of journalism, and "takes no stock," as the
Americans say, in the reptile press. Superbus, for-
tunately, has no wife and children; he has made
other arrangements; but he is a censor of morals,
and you should read his poetry! He dedicated a
volume of sonnets to the successful friend whom he
now traduces—all for the public good, of course, and
he is happy in that belief. Does he look joyful?
Well, it must be confessed that he shambles in his
gait; his shoulders are up to his ears; his face has
a somewhat worn look; his nose has a lofty pose;
but he knows himself and his own merits, and he
lives to proclaim the shocking depravity and shameful
presumption of the men whom the Public have exalted,
while he is still a waiter on fortune. Does that friend
of his early days bear him any malice? Not he.
Does he think that the Arab sentiment of hospitality
should influence a man when he is about to do an
unjust or ungrateful thing to his host? Not he. The
battle of London is a hard one, and the unappreciated
have much to bear. He has suffered, and is still the
good Samaritan. Moreover, he is getting into the

sere and yellow leaf. I heard him comparing notes recently with one of the most generous of men—charitable, benevolent, and of a blameless life—and the good Samaritan's experiences of ingratitude were as nothing compared with those of his friend; but all you have to do, if you are a really good fellow, is not to expect gratitude, and not to allow this blackest of sins in others to influence your generous instincts.

III.

Do I present these commonplace reflections to the readers as part of my own experience? Not at all; I am chatting of friends and their troubles. With you, *mes amis*, I too have suffered; let us hope we are strong. It has been my lot of late to receive some attention from brother newspaper critics, who debit me with journalistic sins I have not committed; but credit me, on the other hand, with feats of skill I have not performed. This is an age of gossip. There are certain columns to be filled. The busy *flâneur* has hard work to keep pace with the alleged appetite of the public for personal notes and criticism. What wonder if the piquant personal critic should now and then have to evolve his facts from his inner consciousness, and his comments from the lees of the wine of forgotten favours!

IV.

"Ah, ah!" exclaims Fox, looking over my shoulder; "you have been hit."

"Not I," is my quick reply.

"Moralising only for the good of the world in general?"

"More or less," I answered.

"You have been hit, I say, and by a man you like, or by one to whom you have been a good friend."

"Perhaps; but what matters!"

"Tell your readers," Fox answers, "if ever they should get stabbed in the dark, or in the open, not with a dagger, but with the sharper weapon of a quill or gold nib, to think of the men they have helped, and they shall find the enemy there; or if the stab is full of the poison of very special personal knowledge, be sure he is an utter stranger to you! It is hardly possible for you, I expect, to believe that I am the subject of much hostile jealousy, not only at Scotland Yard, but in the diplomatic department of Downing Street; fact, I assure you. My little successes in an official way at Berlin and St. Petersburg are affronts to the regular band; my connection with the police is hurled at me as a reason why I degrade the higher walks of diplomacy. And yet I have gone through an apprenticeship in both services, and I don't know that throughout the whole of my career

I have ever stood in another man's way—certainly not with intention and malice aforethought. But as you say, most sensitive and sensible of *littérateurs*, one must not be successful. If by dint of hard work, which is to some men a pleasure, you do get on, perhaps beyond your merits, you must not be thin-skinned, and you must expect the slings and arrows of Envy to come pelting at you. Think of the hard things that are said of men in politics, the best of them—Gladstone, Salisbury, Chamberlain, Hartington.

OUR OLD FRIEND SUPERBUS.

Consider what even they will not say or do in a political contest; fancy the bad taste, even if it is true, of Sir Robert Peel declaring at a Brighton meeting that Lord Beaconsfield told him Mr. Ritchie 'was a pompous ass!'"

V.

Mr. Howells still finds the novel of the future an exciting theme. As if it mattered what the novel of the future may be, or will be, or ought to be. Who cares? Why should any one care? Yet Mr. Howells cannot sleep, it seems, for wondering whether the novel of the future will be a domestic essay or a dramatic narrative. He contends that it ought to be a story without a plot. He says, indeed, with the firmness of an inspired prophet, that it *will* be a story without a plot. Very well, so be it! My idea is that art, in the present, is the great question. The future can take care of itself—if it cannot, why it will not be worth taking care of. And we are all quite satisfied with Mr. Howells's novels; we know they have no plots: but he need not emulate the monkey that had no tail—the adage is somewhat musty. I would not have any one else writing like Howells, even if they could. We don't want all the novelist-world to be writing novels without plots just because Mr. Howells does; why he should desire it is one of the many curious puzzles that afflict the public mind.

VI.

"Howells and James—or Dickens and Thackeray?"

is also an American question of the day it seems. Well, I shall smoke my after-dinner cigarette just as calmly, whether the world at large declares for one or the other or both; and I ask the reader to do likewise. A little tobacco I grant you is useful in these exciting days of the Howells-and-James controversy; for all the trouble seems to come from that quarter. Sometimes I think Howells is laughing in his sleeve and James in his European chambers. And Mr. Howells tells us Scott couldn't write a novel, and that Dickens's " Cricket on the Hearth," and " The Christmas Carol " are false and strained in the pathos, the humour horse-play, the characters theatrical, the joviality pumped, and so on. Very well, that's all right. If Mr. Howells feels it in that way of course there is something wrong with Mr. Howells, and we are all very sorry for him. Everybody on this side asks, " What have we done to Howells ? " for, somehow, people have a habit of thinking that there is always some underlying motive that has nothing whatever to do with the subject ; and the underlying motive is generally considered to be spite or envy or jealousy. But none of these feelings can be influencing Howells ; what he is saying must be the outcome of " pure cussedness " ; he cannot be so utterly devoid of judgment, taste, feeling, sentiment, artistic appreciation, as not really to see the merits of Scott, Dickens, and Thackeray, when he evidently thinks Henry James one of the two finest novelists that ever wrote or will write. "No, sir, it is pure cussedness!"

VII.

It may be jealousy? Nonsense. "A Foregone Conclusion," "The Undiscovered Country," and the two delightful volumes on Venice are almost as well known and read in England as in America; "Daisy Miller" is a standard novel. I have been told that Mr. James does not care for compliments about this work. It is nevertheless one of the most perfect little studies from nature with which I am acquainted; but apart from this Mr. James has a great reputation in England. Bret Harte, as a writer, is a household word on this side; Mrs. Burnett is one of the foremost in the first rank. Mark Twain is as well known as any English humorist. Hawthorne is an English classic. But why continue the list? What is the matter with everything English just now in the eyes of Mr. Howells? Does he want to create an international difficulty? To pass from badinage to seriousness, is not Mr. Howells satisfied with the respectful admiration that has been expressed for the character of Lowell; the unfeigned sorrow felt everywhere in England on account of his death? Surely there is something unfriendly in attacking the literary idols of a people, even a foreign people? We can stand

French authors who see no merit in Shakespeare, that does not trouble us, but we are just as much children in a way as Americans are; we hate to have an American author telling the world that the authors we love are poor creatures, the critics who have praised them asses, the people who read them fools. And what must American readers feel about it? I don't think Howells, James and Lowell are much more read and admired at home than they are in America.

VIII.

The American copyright act is being accepted in a grateful spirit by English authors, whatever may be said to the contrary. One of the first good results will be the publication of plays. I shall be surprised if this does not help largely to revive the age of dramatic literature. For years past it has been a standing rebuke against dramatists, the fact that they have not published their works. But the rebuke has come from an ignorant class of dilettante critics, who have ignored the fact that the publication of a play lost the author the acting rights in America. Copyright being otherwise secured plays are to be printed. This will compel authors to look very strictly after their playing rights nevertheless; but in a year or two practice will make copyright perfect. Pinero and Jones have both had volumes of their plays printed; Dubourg and Grundy will follow. Mr. Pinero's first volume contains *The Profligate*, which has not yet been seen in America, though Mr. Daly secured the rights immediately after its production in London. The Ibsenite play produced some time since in Boston, Mass., the outcome of which is to be an independent theatre, is somewhat on the lines of *The Profligate* as regards plot, but there all similarity ends. *The Profligate* is a literary work; it reads as well as it acts. One of the most poetic of modern English plays is *Charles the First*, by Wills; it is a dramatic poem of a very high order of merit. Wills is an Irishman, and many persons give him credit for a personal motive of hatred of Cromwell in regard to the delineation of that character in the play. But the truth is (though it has never yet been mentioned in print), Colonel Bateman, the famous American manager, insisted upon Wills making Cromwell a villain. "Must have the good man and the bad man in a play," said Bateman; "the hero and the villain, and in this play Cromwell must be the villain." "But," exclaimed Wills, "history, history!" "I don't care a cent about history," said Bateman, "the play, my boy, the play's the thing." And thus Cromwell, played by Belmore, became a villain, and Charles, played by Irving, had all the sympathy and glory that a real dramatic hero should have. Poor old Bateman: he had many great qualities, and with the aid of a fine actor he pulled the Lyceum out of the slough of failure and despond.

His two youngest daughters, Isabel and Virginia, are still touring as "stars" in the English provinces.

IX.

Some years ago I dined at Cyfarthfa Castle with the late Mr. Robert Crawshay. My host was deaf. "I once laid my head against a cathedral organ," he said, "when it had all its power on, and could only hear a faint kind of distant humming." Over our wine (there was a large and distinguished company) Mrs. Rose Mary Crawshay, the host's accomplished wife, handed to some of the gentlemen small scraps of paper and black-lead pencils. They had been there before. "Me too," as the American senator remarked. The good things we had said, or intended to say, we wrote down for the benefit of our deaf but conversational host. After dinner Mrs. Crawshay gathered these scraps of written talk together. Perhaps they were converted into spills. I would rather think, from my knowledge of the gracious hostess, that they are among her treasures to this day; for one of the guests, who had a facile pencil, was a Cabinet Minister, and talked historically about his illustrious chief, Mr. Gladstone. Those manuscript relics of past junketings have, I think, suggested to me the origin of these present after-dinner chats, in black and white, to be gathered up and held together with a clasp of memory. Mr. Crawshay's band of instrumentalists always struck me as a delightful and characteristic incident of self-sacrifice. He could not hear a note; yet his band played regularly on the lawn after dinner. The great ironmaster had a sense of humour. Surely he must sometimes have laughed at those same excellent performers. A band with clever tromboners, fifers, drummers, cymballists, and French-horn blowers in full play must have been a funny spectacle to a deaf man with a sense of humour.

X.

Men who live among stirring events, and are witnesses of historical scenes, often fail to appreciate their importance. I am reminded of this by a remark of J. G. Lockhart to William Allan, when standing before the porch of Abbotsford House, after breakfast, as a brilliant party were about to start on a coursing match. "A faithful sketch of what you at this moment see would be more interesting, a hundred years hence, than the grandest so-called historical picture that you will ever exhibit in Somerset House." In defect of Allan's sketch you will remember that we have Lockhart's masterly pen-and-ink picture, which I have just re-read in Gilfillan's "Life of Sir Walter Scott." I could not help wishing one night a few years back that a great painter could have been present to get inspiration for an historical picture, out of a subject which must have been very suggestive to any artist interested in the stage. The famous original Beefsteak Club-room is part of the premises of the Lyceum Theatre. Mr. Henry Irving, on the night prior to Sarah Bernhardt's departure for the New World, gave a little supper in her honour in this historic room, where Sheridan, Perry, Lord Erskine, Hobhouse, His Grace of Norfolk, and other celebrities were wont to meet. In a recess near the supper table Irving had hung his latest purchase in the way of pictures—a wonderful work, by Clint, of Edmund Kean in the great scene of Sir Giles Overreach. It is full of figures. After supper Irving acted as showman to Sarah Bernhardt and Ellen Terry, telling them the story of the picture, and pointing out the principal portrait studies. What a picture! The three leading players of our time, with Kean and his contemporaries as a background. It was a very interesting night. A paragraph of a few lines recorded it in the press, giving the names of those present—which included the "divine Sarah"; Ellen Terry; Miss Wardell; a lady member of the Bernhardt company; Mr. Comyns Carr, Mr. and Mrs. Savile Clarke, Mr. Bancroft, Mr. J. L. Toole, Mr. Ernest Bendall; Mons. Meyer, Mons. Garnier; and Mr. H. J. Loveday, and Mr. Bram Stoker, members of Mr. Irving's managerial staff. I hope that, some day, one of those present will put the event on record. We may never again see together three such remarkable and interesting artistes as the host

and his two lady guests. Madame Bernhardt came
direct from Her Majesty's Theatre after her night's
performance. She is a great admirer of Irving's
acting, and he of hers. Oddly enough, they are not
unlike each other in appearance; and Edmund Kean
shares with both the same character of forehead and
eyebrows. One is struck with this in Clint's picture.
There is something in physiognomy, depend upon it.
I have more than once been struck with the similarity
of the artistic method of Irving and Sarah Bernhardt.
They are both, to all appearances, utterly unconscious
of their audiences; they both have great moments;
both exercise a certain weird power; both appear to
be weak in physique, and yet are strong, with a remarkable capacity of endurance; both portray death
with singular naturalness; and they possess alike that
magnetic influence over their audiences which is just
the difference between genius and talent.

XI.

The supper table on this memorable occasion was
elaborately decorated with daffodils, China roses, and
narcissus. After the repast, Irving, in a few graceful
words, proposed Madame Bernhardt's health. The
friends around him, he said, were her friends. They
appreciated her genius; they wished her God-speed
in her long and arduous tour. It was a great delight
to him and to them to meet her, and to pay her art

their tribute of admiration. He begged to propose her health, and to wish her a prosperous and happy tour. "I say happy," he said with emphasis, "because money is not everything, and we know you will have a prosperous trip; but we wish you a happy trip, good health, and pleasant circumstances!" The toast was drunk with much cordiality, and the famous guest smiled, and saying, "I thank you very much," nodded appealingly to M. Meyer, her manager, who rose, apologised for Madame's limited knowledge of English, and said how much she appreciated the honour Mr. Irving had conferred upon her. Mr. Toole then proposed the health of "our leading English actress, Ellen Terry," which was heartily drunk, and briefly acknowledged by Miss Terry, who expressed her delight at the tribute which had been paid to Madame Bernhardt.

XII.

When the ladies had retired, and all had heartily wished Sarah *bon voyage* for the last time, we fell to discussing the relative merits of the dramatist and the actor, on which an eminent critic argued that a great interpreter was as much a genius as a great creator. Irving, with his usual modesty, argued that even "the noblest Roman of them all," Edmund Kean, must be regarded as holding a very secondary place to the dramatist. "Leaving Shakespeare out of the question," Knight replied, " No. Kean to-day has a greater fame than any dramatist of his time, as you have in your day. Who will be remembered most in the records of these days—Mathias in *The Bells*, or the author; *Charles the First*, or the author; *Louis XI.*, or the author?" The debate was as interesting as the occasion was memorable. I wish I could picture both for you, as Lockhart pictured the Abbotsford Hunt. I have dwelt on the subject already at greater length than I intended; but the sketch, incomplete though it be, is an exclusive bit of stage history, and that has been held to redeem even the dullest records. It is not easy in these days to see and hear interesting things that are outside the lynx-eyed ken of news collectors and telegraphists, press associations, cable syndicates, and the rest; but now and then the world of London has moments which are not for them.

XIII.

A curious town, London, the Metropolis of an eccentric people. I buy my coals from a marquis. The other day I paid a fare to the guard of an earl's coach. A friend of mine knows the near relation of a duke who drives a cab. Lord Lonsdale was recently the manager of a travelling theatrical company. It came out in a law suit that Sir John Astley and the Duke of Marlborough both keep hansoms, and that in the absence of their owners from London the grooms are allowed to ply for hire with their masters' vehicles and horses. Sir John pays his cab-groom thirty-five shillings a week, and when the baronet is not using his hansom the servant rents it at ten shillings a-day. These revelations were the result of a trial for damages, in which Sir John was mulcted in a hundred odd pounds, because his groom had run into a van and hurt the driver thereof. Sir John's is a fast horse—the groom a fast driver, who, amongst his other achievements, drops the letter "h" in a cheerful and defiant spirit. I wonder if he was the cabby I had dealings with lately? "*Hi! stop! pull up!*" I shouted, after he had twice shaved the wheels of lumbering vans and taken the varnish off a very smart carriage, his horse going like the wind, to the terror of my wife and to my own great alarm. "*Wot's the matter?*" he exclaimed, when at last he had checked his horse's wild career. "*Wot is it?*" I explained that he drove too fast for my wife, and that she wished to get out. "*Wot nonsense!*" he replied. "You should enter your horse for the Derby, or take him to Sanger's and put him in a Roman chariot," I nevertheless suggested. "*Ah!*" he answered, with a sneer, "*you wants a wooden 'oss, you does: that's your style—a wooden 'oss!*" As he trotted away down Portland Place he looked back pityingly to repeat, "*Yes, a wooden 'oss is about your mark!*"

XIV.

But, as I was saying, when you paused to light a fresh cigarette, London is a strange city, full of every kind of possibility—social, criminal, political, romantic. Let me tell you a true story of the day. Until a year ago a certain gentleman wrote for a daily paper. He was an odd sort of person; not very clever, did ordinary work and little of it. His salary was small in proportion. He laboured in the sub-editorial room about an hour a day. Nevertheless, at intervals, he was able to lay aside his pen for whole weeks together. He took long trips beyond the English Channel. In these intervals a substitute of his own appointment took his semi-sub-editorial place in the London newspaper office. The substitute received paragraphs and messages from his chief for the news editors. They were interesting notes on foreign politics, written in a tone of knowledge and authority. Most of them came from Russia. When the occasional writer last went away his substitute received no letter from him, no telegram, no more mysterious bits of Continental news. Weeks passed, months slipped away without a sign. The other day the assistant, under official direction, visited the absent gentleman's rooms, interviewed his landlady, examined his papers, and discovered that the odd gentleman who travelled so much, and wrote so little, was a Russian spy! Beyond this there was a clue which suggested a Nihilistic trap and an assassination. Peace to his ashes!

XV.

"To meet the Count, Countess, and Baron Magri." So ran the legend. It was inscribed on the back of an "At Home" card from Mr. and Mrs. Charles Duval, Langham Street. "Sunday, August 15th, 1886. Music 8 to 12.30." Mr. Duval was the well-known entertainer. He had travelled all over the civilised world—"*and Russia*," as my friend Sutherland Edwards would say. It was a charming reception. Many interesting people were present, and the music—including selections from Handel and Mozart—offended no religious prejudices. The Count, Countess, and Baron were most polite and condescending. They were very little people—dwarfs in fact—and sat on tiny chairs. The Countess was the widow of our once familiar friend, General Tom Thumb. I don't care where they get their patents of nobility from. No doubt they, too, are little ones. What would such small people do with great formal sealed documents? The Count, the Countess, and the Baron were all in faultless evening dress. The little lady, with her little gloved hands and kid-shod feet, her little voice and bright eyes, chatted to me about her travels and her husband, who was not simply a dwarf, but a true man in miniature, a well-proportioned, intelligent little gentleman. He wore

a moustache, and was quite natural to talk to, only
one had to stoop. I hope none of us, dear friends,
may ever stoop to less worthy objects.

XVI.

"Wonderful people!" said Mr. Oscar Wilde, after
contemplating them with a benevolent smile; "depend
upon it, that is the proper size!" Where was I reading the other day some speculations upon the possibilities, or rather the impossibilities, of man, if he had
been no bigger than the monkey?—I forget just now.
One day I will find the volume marked, and then we
will perhaps return to the subject. These little people
whom Mr. and Mrs. Duval introduced to a crowd of
fashionable and artistic people, on Sunday night,
are intelligent, clever, and accomplished. Do you
remember Commodore Nutt? He was a very dignified gentleman, a fop in his dress, a giant in his
amours and pastimes. I played a game of billiards
with him at the Star Club in Worcester, years ago.
Afterwards he lighted a cigar and posed with his
back to the fire, vainly trying to watch the succeeding game. He had stood upon a chair in the combat
with me. It never could have occurred to him that
he was really small. "The mind" was "the measure
of the man" with him, and very properly. A great
hulking son of a local banker came into the room,
stalked up to the fire, and swept the Commodore into

the fender. Happily, he was not big enough to fall into the fire. When he gathered himself together and came at the stranger with angry words and threatening fists, I shall never forget the other fellow's look of surprise. The Brobdingnagian who found Gulliver was not more amazed at the manikin than was the stranger at the miniature gentleman whom he presently looked down upon; for the doors of the local show had not yet been opened. The Commodore received, I need not say, an ample apology, and accepted from his newly-made friend a cigar as long as his arm, which he complacently lighted and smoked over a soda and brandy. It was fortunate that he did not overbalance himself when he lifted the mighty glass to his lips, otherwise our comedy might have ended in a tragedy.

XVII.

Do we ever quite get away from London, even when we try? Not long ago, but prior to the Haymarket management of Mr. Tree, I took a trip through the New Forest to the brightest, prettiest, and sunniest "sea-side" in England. But London was there ahead of me. My first invitation on reaching Bournemouth was to go to the theatre to see Mr. Beerbohm Tree play "Iago" for the first time on any stage; and there behold me hurried away from the smother of London to sit in a theatre at Bournemouth. Mr. Benson and his company of Shakespearians occupied the local stage, and that most creditably. Mr. Tree proved to be as original an "Iago" as Mr. Benson was picturesque as "Othello." Mr. and Mrs. Tree had been hard at work there rehearsing and acting as "stars." When their "day-off" came they drove over to Barcombe Manor and helped Lady Shelley to entertain the shop girls of Bournemouth. The city waiter, you know, whenever he has a holiday, goes to the West End and "helps" another waiter. Mr. and Mrs. Tree and Sir Percy Shelley played a little one-act drama for the amusement of Lady Shelley's friends. A capital movement this bringing together of the classes and the masses. Lady Shelley was giving an "At Home" once a week to a party of Bournemouth shop girls, and both hostess and guests looked forward to those Wednesdays with mutual pleasure. One night Mrs. Tree played "Portia" for the first time, and there was a notable house, which included Lord Edward Somerset, Lady Shelley, Sir Percy Shelley, Mr. Cox, of *The Field*, and how many other distinguished persons I cannot say.

XVIII.

As I step into a comfortable London and South-Western carriage for London, the echoes of the great city seem to be in the air. Parliament has met for an Autumn Session; the Queen has made her speech. Chicago Conventions are threatening us "as with an army on the march." An Academy discussion has drifted into a personal controversy, Mr. Quilter's gage having been picked up by Mr. Andrew Lang. Presently we all bury our heads in the morning papers. The train goes thundering on ; the blue sea fades out, the forest merges into town and city ; and finally the lantern on the Clock Tower at Westminster flashes out its legislative signal. And what a light it is, how far-reaching, sweeping the world, the electric eye of the ship of State dominating an Empire which would be as incomplete without Ireland as without India! The day before I left town I met Mr. Gladstone walking down Regent Street ; the line of his mouth in repose now forms a perfect half-circle ("the downward drag severe," some poet calls it), and his face is a wonderful study of curious lines and pathetic wrinkles. He was walking at a steady, swinging pace, and in his wake there followed at a trot a suburban family—father, mother, and three children—a very scientific-looking minister, and two country sight-seers, who appeared to be under a kind of magnetic influence—weak humanities in the wake of a mesmerist. Well, it is a powerful individuality. I think if the Grand Old Gentleman had turned round and beaten the little party with his stick, they would still have held their way just as faithfully as that other greater party of followers have pursued the Great Liberal Magnet of "these strange degenerate days."

XVII.

"*LET US TAKE A WALK DOWN FLEET STREET.*"

Richardson's Printing Office—Where Dr. Johnson first met Boswell—Famous Names—In the Footsteps of Dickens—Hepworth Dixon and " Ruby Grey"—In the Temple—Law and Revel.

I.

FLEET STREET has strangely altered within the past twenty years. Utility has cleared away nearly all the last relics of the picturesque; but no architectural revision of the street can wipe out its history —no electric lamps ever exorcise the ghosts which imagination conjures up in its courts and alleys, its old houses and its ancient taverns. The footsteps of Shakespeare himself hallow the memories of Shoe Lane, where the *Standard* is now printed. " Rare Ben Jonson" and his friends made merry at their club in Apollo Court. Swift and Addison dined at the

Devil Tavern, the site of which is close by. Hoare's Bank covers the ashes of the old Mitre, but you can stand on the pavement and recall the scene where many of the conversations took place which are set forth in Boswell's "Life of Johnson." The plays of Shakespeare were first published in Fleet Street, and to-day, with the exception of the *Times*, all the great daily newspapers have their offices in this busy region. Cobbett's *Political Register* came out in Bolt Court, where Dr. Johnson lived and predicted the lighting of London by gas. Before he went to live in Bolt Court he occupied the house 7, Johnson's Court, though he compiled most of his dictionary and lost his beloved wife, Tetty, in Gough Square.

II.

It is difficult to get out of Fleet Street, once you begin to think about it, and make notes of the multifarious memories, bookish and personal, journalistic and literary, that crowd upon you. The histories of the taverns, the earliest printing offices, and the newspaper palaces that have arisen upon the ancient sites would fill volumes; and this essay only deals with a passing glance at the Temple. Otherwise the recent death of Mr. Edward Lloyd might furnish one with a remarkable chapter of curious chat and gossip. When I called upon him some years ago in connection with certain magazine articles which I was writing for

A BIT OF THE LIBRARY CHAMBERS.

Harper's, in response to a remark of mine about the historic interest of his offices at 12, Salisbury Court, he said: "Very interesting, yes; this house was Richardson's printing office. In this room he wrote 'Pamela,' and here Oliver Goldsmith acted as his reader." It is the old familiar story. You are treading on historic ground every foot you move in London, historic not in a mere antiquarian sense, nor in the narrow meaning of age being historic, but in the breadth of human interest and universal fame. "I can show you Richardson's lease of these very premises," said Lloyd, and, turning over the deeds which conveyed to him a large extent of the local freeholds, he handed me the parchment. It was a lease dated May 30, 1770, from Mrs. Jennings to Mr. Richardson, and the printer-novelist's signature, by the way, was a bolder one than would seem characteristic of the gentle tediousness of "Pamela."

III.

But by your leave we will quit this busy street for no less classic ground in the Temple. Entering the Inner Temple from Fleet Street, we come face to face with literary history; for here was the shop of Jacob Tonson, the publisher of Pope and Warburton, and at whose place of business they first met. By the way, when we are praising the technical and artistic skill of modern printing, it would be just as well if we looked back to some of the earlier editions of the past; let me at random quote that of "The Works of Mr. Alexander Pope," printed by Bowen for Jacob Tonson at the Shakespeare's Head in 1717. Dr. Johnson lived at No. 1 in this lane of the Inner Temple, renting chambers there from 1760 to 1765. Boswell first called upon him here, having been introduced to him a few days previously by Mr. Davies, the actor, who kept a bookseller's shop in Covent Garden, London.

"He received me," says Boswell, "very courteously; but it must be confessed that his apartment and furniture and morning dress were sufficiently uncouth. His brown suit of clothes looked very rusty; he had on a little old shrivelled unpowdered wig, which was too small for his head; his shirt-neck and knees of his breeches were loose; his black worsted stockings ill drawn up; and he had a pair of unbuckled shoes by way of slippers. But all these slovenly particulars were forgotten the moment he began to talk."

For many years this house was inscribed: "Dr. Johnson's Staircase." It disappeared in 1857 to make room for new sets of chambers.

That he might be near Johnson, Boswell took rooms in Farrar's Buildings, at the bottom of Temple Lane, and Charles Lamb (who was born in Crown Office Row) had chambers at No. 4. Who does not remember his description of them in a letter to Coleridge? "Two rooms on the third floor and five rooms above, with an inner staircase to myself, and all new painted, etc., for £30 a year. Just now it is delicious. The best look backwards into Hare Court, where there is a pump always going—just now it is dry. Hare Court's trees come in at the window, so that it's like living in a garden."

Mr. Timbs, in his chat about the Temple, is careful to tell us that Oliver Goldsmith, when he removed from Gray's Inn, took chambers in the lane, on the then library staircase of the Inner Temple, which he shared with one Jeff's, butler to the society. His neighbour Johnson soon paid him a visit, and went prying about the rooms. Goldsmith grew fidgety, and, apprehending a disposition to find fault, exclaimed, with the air of a man who had money in both pockets: "I shall soon be in better chambers than these!" which harmless bravado drew from Johnson four Latin words implying, "It is only yourself that need be looked for."

Poor "Goldy's" next move was not to better chambers, but to what Dr. Scott called "a miserable garret in a London Court." The doctor was rich, however, and spoke "comparatively," no doubt, for the poet was happy in his new quarters, where he wrote a great deal of his "Animated Nature," his studies of rooks being made from his windows, which commanded the old Temple rookery. Profit as well as credit came from "The Good-natured Man," and he was enabled to gratify his desires for handsome rooms. His ambition, however, did not wander beyond the Temple. He bought chambers in Brick Court, Middle Temple,

"LET US TAKE A WALK DOWN FLEET STREET." 183

No. 2, second floor, on the right-hand side of the staircase.

IV.

Here, in spite of the debts and difficulties that

GOLDSMITH'S TOMB.

followed his pardonable ostentation, Goldsmith gave dinner-parties to Johnson, Reynolds, Barry, Bickerstaff, and others, and disturbed his neighbours with his evening romps and dances.

On April 4, 1774, at five o'clock in the morning, poor "Goldy" died. "On the stairs of his chambers there were the lamentations of the old and infirm, and the sobbing of women—poor objects of his charity, to whom he had never turned a deaf ear, even when he was himself struggling with poverty."

The names of Johnson and Goldsmith are perpetuated in the lane by Johnson and Goldsmith buildings, and the Author of "The Vicar of Wakefield" takes his everlasting rest in the shadow of Temple Church. Who is not familiar with that simple slab on the north side of the burial ground which marks the sacred spot, with the words: "Here lies Oliver Goldsmith"?

As you stand and gaze upon this mortuary record you may almost hear the plash of the fountain which Charles Lamb tells us, in " Essays of Elia," he " made it to rise and fall many times, to the astonishment of the young urchins, my contemporaries, who, not being able to guess at its recondite machinery, were almost tempted to hail the wondrous work as magic." Miss Landon has paid poetic tribute to its refreshing and suggestive music.

> "The fountain's low singing is heard on the wind,
>   Like a melody bringing sweet fancies to mind;
>   Some to grieve, some to gladden; around them they cast
>   The hopes of the morrow, the dreams of the past;

"Away in the distance is heard the vast sound,
From the streets of the city that compass it round,
Like the echo of fountains, or ocean's deep call,
Yet that fountain's low singing is heard over all."

I am not sure that the almost primitive fountain of Lamb's days was not a more picturesque incident of the quietude of Fountain Court than the present one.

Do you not remember how Ruth Pinch discovered, as she listened to the music of the Temple fountain, that she had given her heart to John Westlock?

v.

It has not been given to any other author to people London with such reality of fictitious creation as Dickens. The highways and byways of the town are full of them. They meet you at Charing Cross. You find them in the Adelphi Arches. All about Covent Garden you walk in their footsteps. They are in the City, at the West End, in Lincoln's Inn. Bleak House opens in Bell Yard; thence you may reach Fleet Street. Tellson's Bank has changed, Temple Bar has gone; but Mr. Cruncher remains. "Our chambers were in Garden Court," wrote Mr. Pip. And so you travel on to Pump Court with Tom Pinch, to Paper Buildings with Sir John Chester, to King's Bench Walk with Sydney Carton, and back again you ramble into Fleet Street, to find Bradley Headstone watching Eugene Wrayburn; then you have a business trace of Dickens at the *Daily News* office, and get once more into the society of his never-dying creations at the *Cheshire Cheese* with Darnay and Carton, to find other characters beckoning you farther a-field, whither, however, you may not at the moment journey. Scott has done for Edinburgh what Dickens has done for London. Reade relieved some of the gloomiest shadows of Sheffield with the romantic light of "Put Yourself in His Place." Mr. Blackmore has almost given a new name to the district he has painted in his best work. It is called the Lorna Doone country. George Eliot did not adopt real names in describing places. Many a Midland town and village would be classic ground in the eyes of her admirers had she done so. It was left for Dickens to annex London. The cultured American visiting the metropolis for the first time hunts up the localities where the familiar characters of Dickens lived, moved, and had their being, as assiduously as he examines the historic relics of Westminster and the Tower.

VI.

Some years ago I met, in an evidently reflective mood, one of the most eloquent of that stronghold's historians, prowling about the Temple. "A new history of the haunts of Law?" I asked. "No, a novel, sir. I am going to try my hand at fiction." It was Hepworth Dixon. He was mapping out the scenes of "Ruby Grey," a story which later demonstrations of Fenianism ought to have revived into popularity. The central action of the drama was the Clerkenwell explosion (since then represented upon

THE FOUNTAIN.

the stage of the Adelphi in a play by Mr. Pettitt called *A Fight for Life*), and Dixon was scrupulous in naming the localities in which his characters were introduced. He was delighted to have found near Clerkenwell a "Cut Throat Lane"; and close by the spot where I met him Ashen Tree Court and Wilderness Lane, carrying one back to the days of tie wigs, sedan chairs, and footpads. How pleasantly he gossiped about Charles Lamb and the old days of the Temple, I recall now that he is gone. He was a barrister-at-law, wore several foreign decorations, had made a reputation as editor of the *Athenæum*, and author of " New America"; but the one distinction of which he was really proud was that of being a Justice of the Peace.

VII.

" Pendennis " introduces us to the Temple, and Thackeray speaks of the " rough comforts and freedom of those venerable inns which have the *Lamb and Flag* and the *Winged Horse* for their ensigns." As in the past, so in the present, literary London has quarters in the Temple, better quarters in most respects than in the past, and, in some instances, luxurious rooms furnished in the best manner, and waited upon by obsequious attendants. Briefless barristers and advocates known to fame send forth, from the solemn portals of the Temple, manuscripts that are eagerly welcomed by editors in the adjacent streets, where the giant Steam is everlastingly driving the wheels of the greater giant Journalism. Literature is the luxury of these writers; newspaper work their necessity. Mr. Briefless will make as much in a week by chatty paragraphs for the society Press as the essayists of Addison's days received for their work in a twelve-month; and the practised leader-writer who is on the staff of a great daily could live in the Temple like a gentleman, without thinking of legal fees. But work of this kind is not literature proper, though it is the pecuniary reward of writing for the Press that has enabled the best authors of modern days to devote some of their most cherished hours to *belles lettres*. Mr. Burnand studied for the bar and was called. He wrote for the Press and the stage, and is now editor of *Punch*. Mr. W. S. Gilbert burned the midnight oil in the Temple, where he probably wrote "Bab Ballads" on his brief paper, and sketched his first plays while mastering the first principles of English jurisprudence. He has not shown any more reverence for the wig and gown, and the *Lamb and Flag* and the *Winged Horse*, than the anonymous wit who burlesqued these ancient arms of the two societies of the Temple. They inspired a rhymer as follows :—

> " As by the Templar's haunts you go,
>   The Horse and Lamb display'd
> In emblematic figures show
>   The merits of their trade.
>
> " That clients may infer from thence
>   How just is their profession ;
> The Lamb sets forth their innocence,
>   The Horse their expedition.

"O happy Britain, happy isle!
  Let foreign nations say,
'Where you get justice without guile,
  And law without delay!'"

Upon this the W. S. Gilbert or the Henry Leigh of the period wrote:—

"Deluded men these holds forego,
  Nor trust such cunning elves.
These artful emblems tend to show
  Their *clients*—not *themselves*.

"'Tis all a trick; these all are shams,
  By which they mean to cheat you;
But have a care, for *you're* the *lambs*,
  And they—the *wolves* that eat you!

"Nor let the thought of 'no delay'
  To these their courts misguide you;
For *you're* the showy horse, and they
  The *jockeys* that will ride you."

Perhaps it is a fortunate thing that by the help of journalism many lawyers are enabled to get along without clients, whereby some of the lambs escape with their lives, if not with their wool, the wolf finding other food than mutton.

VIII.

So lasting and continuing are the literary associations of the Temple, that while mentioning Gilbert (did not Talfourd write *Ion* in the Temple?) one pauses to note that Sir Christopher Hatton and four other students of the Inner Temple wrote the play of *Tancred and Gismund*, which in 1568 was acted by that society before Queen Elizabeth; and there is a copy (1592) among the Garrick plays in the British

TEMPLE CHURCH.

Museum. The Temple has always been associated more or less with plays and players. It kept one of its festivals a few years ago by assembling in its great hall to hear Mr. Brandram read one of

Shakespeare's plays. "The Revels," so-called, came to an end in 1723, when plays were enacted—*Love for Love* by Congreve, a Templar, and *The Devil to Pay* by a company of actors from the Haymarket. "The Master of the Revels formed a ring and danced, or rather walked, round the fireplace three times, the old song of 'Round about the Coal Fire,' with music, being sung by Toby Aston, dressed in a bar-gown. Dancing followed, in which the ladies (who had been spectators of the play from the gallery) joined; then a collation and more dancing. The then Prince of Wales was present in the music gallery *incog*." There has been in recent days a modern "Revel" in the Temple, originated and conducted by Mr. Arthur à Beckett, but to-day in these classic quarters work eclipses play. Law is the rule, Revel the exception.

Under the very roof where the benchers and their friends listened to Mr. Brandram's reading, *Twelfth Night, or What You Will* was played in the lifetime of its immortal author. "Yes," says Charles Knight, "the actual roof under which the happy company of benchers, barristers, and students listened to that joyous and exhilarating play—full of the truest and most beautiful humanities, fitted for a season of cordial mirthfulness—exists, and it is pleasant to know that there is one locality remaining where a play of Shakespeare was listened to by his contemporaries, and that play *Twelfth Night*."

XVIII.

FROM THE GRIFFIN TO COVENT GARDEN.

Glimpses of the Strand—Where Dr. Johnson Worshipped—Editors of *Punch*—Jumbo and Chunee—Past and Present—Historic Streets—Mrs. Lirriper and Sir Roger de Coverley.

I.

FROM the Temple to Covent Garden is a ten minutes' walk; yet, if you pause to think of its historic landmarks, or even to take a stranger's interest in what is passing around you, the journey may be a long one. The Griffin, with the strange eventful history of its site, first challenges you; then the Law Courts, and next the Church of St. Clement Danes; and if you are of a morbid turn you may try and find a relic of Lyons Inn, but the last vestige of the quaint old place that was entered from the Strand disappeared in 1880. Its modern history is associated with the murder of Weare, the gambler, by Thurtell, commemorated in the street ballad of the time:—

> "They cut his throat from ear to ear,
> His brains they battered in;
> His name was Mr. William Weare
> He dwelt in Lyons Inn."

The reader who prefers to walk in less sanguinary footsteps will turn with Mr. Augustus C. Hare as his literary guide into the Church of St. Clement Danes, where Dr. Johnson was a worshipper. A brass plate marks the pew in the north gallery where he sought "how to purify and fortify his soul, and hold real communion with the Highest." It was in this church that, in 1676, "Sir Thomas Grosvenor was married to Miss Mary Davies, the humble heiress of the farm now occupied by Grosvenor Square and its surroundings, which have brought such enormous wealth to his family."

II.

When Mark Lemon, the first editor of *Punch*, the author of hundreds of songs and many popular plays, was compiling his volume entitled "Up and Down the London Streets," I walked with him over much of the ground, more especially that between Fleet Street and Covent Garden. I remember that he halted as we left the Temple to recall the revels of the lawyers in the olden days, and to regret that so much of the picturesque in life had gone out of our English manners and customs. He was an odd mixture of business acuteness and sentimentality. He rejoiced in the fashions of old ideas, took a delight in Christmas festivities, had the true social instinct, was a Bohemian of that better world of Bohemia

outside gin, sawdust, and clay pipes. He found as
much delight in getting out *Punch's* annuals as the

ST. CLEMENT DANES.

readers ever felt in sliding their paper-knives through
the merry publication by the side of winter fires
He was for many years a well-known figure in Fleet

Street; his portly form and his lion-like head, with its silky white hair, were often seen in Covent Garden Market; his favourite tavern was in that region, and his London chambers were in Bedford Street.

In the Strand my genial companion repeated the observation of Shirley Brooks (who was his second successor on *Punch*), "It is a liberal education to walk down the Strand." Fleet Street was Dr. Johnson's favourite walk; Shirley Brooks preferred the Strand, and pronounced it "the pleasantest and handsomest street in London."

It could at any rate be truly said that Shirley Brooks was one of the handsomest men that ever walked there—tall, straight, a free yet distinguished manner, a pleasant, open, frank face, with large bright eyes and brown hair that curled in the manner of the statues of Hercules. He adorned every branch of literature in which he exercised his pen; his novels and his plays were the work of a conscientious and cultured author. He wrote verse with the grace of a man of taste and feeling. His satire had the polish of a delicate wit; and one cannot pay Mr. Lucy a higher compliment than to say that as *Punch's* Parliamentary historian his weekly record is not altogether unworthy of his brilliant predecessor.

III.

Passing Essex Street my friend recalled the fact

that here, at the house of Lady Primrose, the Young Pretender paid his secret visit to London in 1760, and that in the same street Flora Macdonald found a

A BIT OF THE STRAND.

refuge; while at the Essex Head Dr. Johnson established a club which Boswell and his friends kept up for years after his death.

Norfolk Street and Arundel Street started up innumerable ghosts, memories of the romances of history and of fiction. Mrs. Lirriper lived in Norfolk Street, and the *Spectator* records how Sir Roger de Coverley gave the Mohocks the slip at the corner. Peter the Great was lodged in a house at the bottom of the street near the river; and later, William Penn, the famous founder of Pennsylvania, lived in the same house. Here are texts for the romantic thinker and ready writer. To him I leave these tempting subjects for the present. Peter the Great would lead one a tremendous dance. You find his footsteps all over this locality and up in the City. His boat was always awaiting him by the Strand. There were palaces along the river in those days that might have reminded travellers of the Grand Canal. Close by, in Howard Street, Captain Hill, in a duel, slew Mr. Mountfort for love of the good and virtuous Mrs. Bracegirdle, "the Diana of the Stage."

IV.

Speaking of old Somerset House and the apartments there, which had not been opened for a hundred years when William Chambers visited them preparatory to the erection of the present building, Mark Lemon said he thought a capital way to tell the story of a hundred years of the past life of London would be to describe a representative man of the time falling asleep in his room, waking up *à la* Rip Van Winkle, and then going forth to note "the changes between now and then." The idea—not set forth as particularly original—grew out of the fact that Sir William "walked through rooms where feet had not intruded for nearly a hundred years, amid mouldering walls, broken casements, crumbling roofs, and decaying furniture. A chandelier still depended from the ceiling of one of the rooms, and velvet curtains, tawny with age, fringed with a few shreds of gold and spangles, hung in tatters about the dingy windows. In another room there were broken couches and tattered hangings, screens, sconces, fire-dogs, and the vestiges of a throne."

"Rare Ben Jonson" lived in Hartshorne Lane, Strand, "and went to a private school in St. Martin's Church before he became a Westminster boy." In September, 1823, a leaden coffin was discovered placed in the ground perpendicularly. At the top of the narrow grave was a square stone bearing the initials "B. J." Inquiry led to the unearthing of a tradition among the old men of the Abbey that when Ben Jonson was very ill he was asked, supposing he did not recover, where he would like to be buried. "In Westminster Abbey, if I can get a foot of ground there." At the poet's death application was made to the Dean on the strength of this expressed wish, and the venerable ecclesiastic took Ben at his word, and gave sufficient ground to bury him standing. The skeleton, wonderfully preserved, of the deceased bore out the story.

When he first came to London, Dr. Johnson lodged

COVENT GARDEN.

and had his dinner in Exeter Street, Strand, for 4½d a day, "he and Garrick having borrowed £5 on their joint note from Mr. Wilcox, the bookseller."

Apropos of "Jumbo" of Anglo-American fame, it

is interesting to note that at old Exeter Change, Strand, "Chunee," the great elephant of the previous half-century, was exhibited. His skeleton may be seen to this day at the College of Surgeons. Says Mark Lemon: "Chunee once appeared at Drury Lane Theatre in a pantomime, to the great disgust of the property man of the rival house, who said, 'I should be very sorry if I could not make a better elephant than *that*.'"

V.

There have been wonderful changes in the Strand even since Mark Lemon passed away. "Up and Down the London Streets" contains no mention of the Griffin nor the Law Courts. Temple Bar still stood alone in its glory—when we walked out of the Temple—to emphasise Johnson's remark about the heads which decorated it when he and Goldsmith first made its acquaintance: "Perhaps our ashes may mingle with theirs." Since Mark's day there has been serious talk of pulling down the two fine churches that carry on the architectural beauties of Fleet Street and the Strand away to St. Paul's. The Tivoli has sprung up within a few months, and the Gaiety Restaurant and other similar places of refreshment seem to the younger generation to be almost hoary with time, and the *Cock* a mere tradition; yet a few years ago, when I walked the bounds of his book with Mark Lemon, we dined at the *London* by Temple Bar; we lunched at the *Rainbow*; and we supped at the *Cock*. The grill-room, as we know it to-day, was an institution to come. Nor had the taxes been

SOMERSET HOUSE, FROM THE EMBANKMENT.

taken off knowledge. The stamp duty was still imposed on newspapers.

Mark Lemon remarked that the Strand was not always the handsome thoroughfare that Shirley Brooks thought it. In the time of the unfortunate

Edward II. it was a common road, the footway overrun with thickets and bushes, unpaved until the days of Henry VIII., when the landowners between Charing Cross and Strand Cross were compelled to make a good road and build three bridges—"one at Strand Bridge Lane, another at Ivy Bridge Lane, and a third eastward of St. Clement's Church."

VI.

Referring to a recent controversy as to the last resting-place of Oliver Cromwell, it may be interesting to mention that the Protector's body lay in state at Somerset House, "the folly and profusion" of which ceremony is said to have so provoked the people that they threw dirt on the escutcheon placed over the Somerset House gate. "The funeral," says Lemon, "cost about £28,000, but with this Cromwell could have nothing to do, and so the live asses kicked at the dead lion." It was once said that Cromwell's last resting-place was in Red Lion Square, under a stone obelisk which formerly stood in the centre of that out-of-the-world place.

Go on towards Charing Cross, and you will have material enough for a hundred such pages as the one you are glancing at, and food for years of contemplation. If it is not the handsomest of all the London streets, the Strand is endowed with the most ancient and romantic associations; while at Charing Cross you stand in the centre of London, and for the great business of the world's life in the very centre of the universe. But our destination is Covent Garden. We pass along Southampton Street, noted in current history for the fact that here phosphorus was first manufactured in England. And presently we are in Covent Garden, about which any one might write a volume and still leave something worth saying unsaid. As far back as 1222 this space was the convent garden of Westminster, under the name of Frere Pye Garden. Some 200 years ago the market was held under the shade of a grotto of trees hanging over the walls of Bedford House grounds. In the time of Charles II. it was one of the most pleasant lounges in town. It is under the Bedfords that the entire space has been usurped by the market and transformed into anything but a pleasant or fashionable lounge. When I say it is not a pleasant quarter I do not desire to discount the delight that is to be found in that central corridor of the market building, where fruit and flower shops make an arcade of lovely form and colour and an avenue of sweet perfumes. That little collection of shops, huddled together with a curious disregard of the picturesque and the useful, eclipsed as a market avenue by many provincial cities, is probably unequalled for its stores of rare fruits and its bouquets of choice flowers. The dealers in this insignificant passage, for which the Duke of Bedford takes an enormous rent, have customers all over the world. One of them supplied, and probably does now, the Imperial table at St. Petersburg with English hot-house grapes, peaches, nectarines, pines, and plums. The Imperial Master of all the Russias does not object to Jewish money, nor to the luxuries the Jewish traders collect for the Imperial palace. But this is only a passing chat, a mere hint of the historic and other interesting landmarks that crowd the way in the merest stroll from Temple Bar to Covent Garden.

Scrappy as it is, "without form and void," as the critical reader may suggest, it nevertheless carries pictures that may fill the void, and induce the general reader to walk in the same. How many thousands pass and repass the Strand entrance to Somerset House without a thought as to its history! How many only know Covent Garden as a market!

XIX.

IN THE DEPARTMENT OF CALVADOS.

From London to Caen—A Feast of Lanterns—Pictures at Midnight and After—*La Voiture de M. Cabieux*—The Onion Fair—Cities and their Physiognomy—The Splendid Confusion—"Challenged at the Grave"—A Terrible Story.

I.

SUPPOSING our desires could be gratified without an interval between the wish and its realisation, there would soon be an end to the world's capacity for providing us with enjoyment. Those ill-starred individuals of romance who have been endowed with the prompt realisation of their wishes, have invariably found the fairy gift an undesirable inheritance. Half the pleasure of possession goes in the anticipation and hope that preceded it. We should soon wish for the eternal rest of the grave if our desires were consummated as soon as they are conceived. To hope is to live, to look forward is to be happy. Ask the young with what enjoyment they contemplate the day when they will go forth to see the world. Ask the old why they look back to find their pleasures in memory. The other day I had not seen Caen, the chief town of the department of Calvados, the burial-place of William the Conqueror, and the scene of Beau Brummell's last hours. William and Beau Brummell! What a text for a rebuke to human vanity. The tomb of one and the death of the other are both facts in the

history of Caen. It had been the dream of many years, my sojourn in Caen. I had stood by Niagara, I had

supped in an Indian's wigwam in far-off valleys beyond
Quebec; but Caen was still a tender hope unrealised,
a sunny spot in my untravelled future. Its grey
stone houses, its graceful spires and towers, its lancet
windows, its reminiscences of the Conqueror, its
atmosphere of classic repose, its foreign ways, its
dreamy suburbs; had I not longed to compare them
with our English cities, with Durham, and York,
and Lincoln, and Worcester, and all the quiet rook-
haunted places which still make England a paradise
for the poet, the painter, and the recluse? Black-
burn's "Normandy Picturesque," had revived an old
longing. The church of St. Pierre and the street
of St. Jean, the Calvados caps, and the old-fashioned
habits of the people (if they will forgive what some
may regard as an aspersion on the progressive instincts
of Caen) again set my mind running on Caen.

II.

It has been said that "the fascination of adventure
and hazard forms one of the most powerful spells in
human feeling." This is borne out by the perilous
adventures of mountain climbers in Switzerland, and
English sportsmen in Western America. The chamois
hunters of the Alps are said to be unable to forego
their daring sport even with the full prospect of death
before them. A visit to Caen, if you go by way of

Southampton and Havre, is not altogether devoid of
the excitement of peril and the sensation of adventure.
You may experience the wildest anxieties and suffer
the torments of Hades any stormy night between the
Solent and the shores of St. Adresse. Battles with
porters on the quay may succeed the night's fight
with the ocean, and the delays and uncertainties of
Normandy railways may supply the place of the more
formidable troubles of the Alps and the Prairies before
you land at the chief capital of Calvados, which boasts
not only its own railway proper, but a *chemin de fer
de Caen à la mer*—a rhyming description that Mark
Twain, who "punched in presence of the passengaire,"
would have fully appreciated. But when you go to
Caen may you reach it as I did, a wanderer, unexpected,
unannounced, with all your family impedimenta at
your back. This is not a malicious wish, I assure
you. May you, I repeat, arrive late at night, like
the traveller in the ancient play, with all your family
at your back, and be told that the *fêtes* are on, that
it will not be possible to find one bed, let alone four.
"My dear sir, it is the *fêtes* and races; the town is
crowded; it is very sad that you should not have made
your arrangements beforehand." So it is, but we
are the only passengers nevertheless. We have an
omnibus all to ourselves. Jean will take us to the
leading hotel first? With pleasure. Of course he
will. Failing accommodation there, he will drive us

to all the other houses? Certainly he will. Those bright franc pieces, what passports they are! May you come upon Caen, I say, just as we did. A calm night of autumn. The moon sailing aloft in a blue world. Streets crowded with people. Streets lighted with ten thousand lamps. Streets bright with banners. Streets in which only the omnibus occupied the roadway. Chinese lanterns, like M. Tadema's Regent's Park garden on a reception night, multiplied by thousands; coloured glass lamps that would have reminded Beau Brummell of romps at Bath and gay doings at Ranelagh; gas jets that link to-day with the times of Louis XIV., and mottoes that join "Progress" with the *Courses de Caen*. Above this the picturesque roofs, above them the tower and steeple of St. Pierre. They had lighted a pan of green fire at the back of the church. I am not an architect. If I were, I think I should not have objected to the strange weird light playing for a moment upon that Gothic *façade* and suddenly leaving it in a transient darkness, from which the calm moonbeams presently relieved it. Blunder on, Monsieur Jean; call to thine horse and crack thy whip, it matters little to us how far we journey through scenes like these. Halt! We pull up under a wreath of flags that show their "red, white, and blue" in a blaze of lanterns. There is a band of music. It heads a torchlight procession. The Marseillaise, with

cymbals and drum, crashes and wails, pent up between
the tall grey houses. Tramp, tramp, tramp, come
the soldiers. They are Norman and Bretagne troops.
A vast crowd follows them, taking up the stirring
music of the band with voices loud and strong, and
marching in the lurid light of torch and lantern.
The Marseillaise! What ghosts the thrilling hymn
invokes! One above all others: it is a fair and
lovely woman. "She is of stately Norman figure; in
her twenty-fifth year; of beautiful, still countenance;
her name is Charlotte Corday, heretofore styled
D'Armans, while Nobility still was." She rises out
of her secluded stillness. She moves out of the dim
ferment of Caen. Presently she is in the drowsy
diligence, lumbering along towards Paris. In due
course, going straight to its purpose, this sublime
figure is face to face with Destiny. "Citoyen Marat,
I am from Caen, the seat of rebellion, and wish to
speak with you." Anon there is a cry: "A moi,
chère Annie. Help, dear!" What a grim tragedy
it is! In three acts—two that are terrible. How the
lightning pen of Carlyle fills in the dialogue and the
pictures! Act III.: She stands before the execu-
tioners. A young, fair creature, with a still calm
smile and a maidenly blush on her face. And then——
But move on again, good Jean. Crack thy whip.
Exorcise that poor ghost of Terror. Good, friend Jean.
On again, good Jean. We have arrived. To be

sure, the grand hotel of the Place Royal is very full. They have turned hundreds away. While we are discussing the situation, some provincials are joking each other about having to sleep in the stables. But we are English. It is even suspected that we are Americans. Madame, who jingles her keys as she condoles with us on the difficulties of the situation, will do her best for us. All their charges are, of course, doubled during the *fêtes*. That we are quite prepared for, we say. "Thank you, Jean. Yes, bring in the luggage." I recur to that wish in your behalf, *mon ami*; may you see Caen as I saw it. There are balconies to those chambers that overlook the Place Royal, balconies and French windows; and at night the murmur of the streets comes up to you like a distant voice, and in the morning you are on a level with the clocks that beat out the hours one after the other so lazily, that they seem to dally with Time, and draw it out into long, shadowy minutes.

III.

At midnight the last fragments of the crowd gathered together to extinguish their torches and make their good nights. As the clock struck they were leaving the Place Royal. Not a soul of them

drunk. In London gin and swipes would have put
these fag-ends of the procession by the ears, and laid
the rest by the heels. Even the old cathedral cities
I have enumerated would have heard the howling of
tipsy revellers. All night; and the next day the
police charges would have been many and sad. Lager
beer is the salvation of New York. I suspect the
mild beer and cider of Caen have something to do
with the phenomenon just mentioned. We like better
in England our "strong waters." Gin and whiskey
are the twin curses of the British Empire. I looked
out upon Caen the next morning at six. The men
who had sung and marched the night before were
wending their way to work, their *sabots* invoking
the echoes of the otherwise silent streets. Burnt out
Chinese lanterns flapped to and fro in the morning
breeze, and the city clocks, with a pleasant disagree-
ment, struck the hour. The old houses lifted their
ornamental gables to the sky. Flags and streamers
made patches of colour against the grey stone of the
streets. The repose of the scene was intensified by
contrast with the glare and brightness and festal
shouts of the previous night. Then I fancy there is
always a peculiar charm in looking down upon a city
without mixing with the people, getting the picture
of it in your mind without locomotion, seeing it
through a window, and feeling that you are outside
all its social and human influences. Cowper conveys

something of what I mean in his own beautiful and
poetic way when he says :—

> "'Tis pleasant, through the loopholes of retreat,
> To peep at such a world ; to see the stir
> Of the great Babel, and not feel the crowd ;
> To hear the roar she sends through all her gates
> At a safe distance, where the dying sound
> Falls a soft murmur on the ear."

IV.

Not that Caen ever "roars." She is gentle as the first footsteps of summer. They go on their way, the people of Caen, with unobtrusive tread, slipping into some old church now and then to say a prayer. There is an influence of calm in the air. You rest while you walk at Caen. And yet they talk of progress and liberty and other stirring things, and if you take up the local "Itinéraire du Chemin de Fer Caen à la Mer," you find quite a spirited account of the march which Caen is making with the other great cities of Christendom. The pilgrims who journeyed, thirty years ago, on the road from Caen to La Délivrande, and having finished their onions at the Petit Enfer, never suspected that a day would come when a steam engine, pulling along large trucks, would carry bathers from Caen to the shore of Luc in an hour. How much more graphically this little French guide tells its story than would any similar handbook in England. It is quite a literary performance in its way. Let us pick out the brief retrospect of travelling, thirty years ago and now, from the well-printed and nicely annotated pages. It seems, then, that the only means of transport which existed at that time was a sort of light dog-cart, which is not yet forgotten by those who used to risk their lives in this whimsical conveyance. A true type of the antediluvian coach, the carriage of M. Cabieux, was a box of a rectangular form and divided into two parts—the interior a place of torture, the exterior a *coupé* open to the rain, the dust, and the wind; the whole covered with a cart tilt, patched and mended. In the front, on a chair covered with straw, was seated the driver, vainly endeavouring to excite two wretched screws with his shouts and his whip. On leaving Caen the equipage left behind it—

> "Dans un chemin montant, sablonneux, malaise
> Et de tous les côtés au soleil exposé,"

and took its way towards La Délivrande with a nonchalance which was impressive. This vehicle has been superseded, this rough and sandy road has been completely transformed. Instead of *la voiture de M. Cabieux*, the highway from June to September is busy with breaks, dog-carts, Américaines, and barouchés, interspersed with little omnibuses belonging to the various towns, with banners waving in the breeze.

V.

In the first days of September this procession of holiday makers on the road from Caen to the sea gives place to one of an entirely different character. From Luc, Langrune, Lion, Douvres, come carts and wagons of all descriptions to the fair which is held at Caen St. Michael's Day, and devoted to the sale of the onion. This vegetable is an important product of this part of the coast, and the onion fair at Caen has its prototype in the famous fairs of Nottingham and Birmingham of the English midlands. The Caen fair dates back to a high antiquity. Granted by William the Conqueror to the Abbé of St. Etienne, it was first held on St. Laurent's Day, but this feast clashing with wheat harvest, it was transferred in the sixteenth century to the present fixture. De Bras relates that in 1461 "Ambroise de Lore, a Norman knight, made a great enterprise at a fair which was held at the Bourg l'Abbé. With 700 horsemen he took all the English merchants, and caused several to be killed." My little friend, the "Itinéraire," adds: "This knight took off as well all the goods exposed for sale, and hereby conformed to the practical spirit of his countrymen." Those persistent English traders, how dearly they have paid for the shop-keeping proclivities of the race in all ages and in all lands! This fair of St. Michael was formerly held in the close of Benvrelu, where now stands the new railway station. In those days were to be seen, pell-mell, bags of onions, turnips, pears, apples, beasts and people. In the midst of an indescribable din, there the merchants transacted their business. In the Norman inns, with their large rooms decorated with old tapestry, circulated great flagons of cider. Sometimes numerous casks were broached in the open air, giving forth copious streams of the Norman nectar, which men and women quaffed with equal gusto; the women in cotton bonnets or head-dresses of white handkerchiefs, the fichus crossed on the neck; the men in blue blouses, with their whips passed round their necks. These, with a crowd of barefooted children, groups of "ambulating merchants," and strings of cattle, must have made up a fine old Flemish picture. On the next day, under the dews of October, it was not an uncommon sight to see the swineherd and his pupil in a paternal embrace. Even in these modern days, and notwithstanding my experience of that first night of the *fêtes*, the evening after the feast of St. Michael has some curious scenes for remembrance on the road home, the onion merchants meeting *en route* companies of brothers coming back to Caen with the first cold winds of the autumn. *Les traces pasans* return in disorder, holding in their hands either a large lantern fixed on a pole, or a candle covered with an oil-paper shade, and tipsily affected by copious draughts of Calvados brandy.

"One may see their lanterns stop instinctively before every wayside inn."

VI.

One of the most ancient cities of Europe, Caen has no equal in respect of its examples of Gothic buildings. It is difficult to think of any city at the moment that offers such peculiar attractions to an Englishman. Something akin to his own ancient cities, it is yet altogether different in its general physiognomy, if one may speak of the physiognomy of a town. Julian Hawthorne, who has, no doubt, inherited his poetical power of motive analysis from his father, thinks it is with communities as with individuals: "Men are a kind of hieroglyphic writing, hard to decipher; but they translate themselves into their houses, and we may read them there at leisure." Judged by this standard the people of Normandy are not a cleanly race of people. Their back doors open upon an atmosphere of bad odours. In singular contrast, and to be credited in their favour, is the order and sweetness of their kitchens. This develops an incongruity of character which requires careful study to comprehend. But if the men of Caen are to be estimated according to their building arrangements they are an enviable people. If their walls and pavements and roadways are but the incarnation of the true city which primarily inheres in the brains and wills of the citizens, then indeed may we sit at the feet of those sober men of Caen and learn. Swedenborg says cities represent doctrines. Caen is then symbolical of a calm, settled faith in the god of popes and priests, and troubles itself no further with controversy. All is finished at Caen—there is no room for change. It is a lusty old man who has worn buckled shoes and patches, now in modern dress, clean, white-haired, hearty, and full of reminiscences of good wine and pleasant friends. On the score of cleanliness and convenience, Caen might be considered a modern city, and yet we walk here in the footsteps of William the Conqueror and his brother Rufus. It presents none of the dilapidations which some old English cities show, though its Abbayes aux Hommes et aux Dames were founded eight hundred years ago. The streets are in better order than any other French provincial city I have visited. Only once in a way does that offensive odour which is so common to the Continent of Europe invade the air. The conduits and fountains that supply the citizens with fresh water are turned on at intervals into the gutters, and thence flush the sewers. This old-fashioned method must have many advantages. At all events it is pleasant. Who that knows the lovely old city of Wells, in England, does not find in his memory the cheerful trickle of the water that irrigates the old streets? Then how much better one can understand the adventures of Andersen's tin soldier with these street torrents in one's mind. Caen is well paved and lighted. The houses, full of picturesque examples of Gothic architecture, are built of the stone which was used in the construction of the Tower of London, and which in the olden days of warfare was "respected" at sea by the English cruisers. Time has softened the colour of the stone, and brought the streets into the same grey hues as the churches. The windows are fitted with exterior shutters familiar in American and Continental cities, and popular at Brighton and Ramsgate on our own side of the water.

VII.

But where, except perhaps at Rouen, shall we look for the turrets and pinnacles and the splendid confusion of the Gothic method which characterises the city of Caen? As in painting, so it is in architecture —beauty depends on light and shade. In buildings this is obtained by the bays or projections in the surface. "If," says an authoritative writer on the subject, "these tend to produce horizontal lines, the building must be deemed Grecian, however whimsically the doors and windows may be constructed. If, on the contrary, the shadows give a preference to perpendicular lines, the general character of the building will be Gothic." The shadows at Caen can hardly be said to be consulted as to the "preference." They fall here and there in deep patches, and here and there in long, dark shafts. They tempt you into picturesque archways; they seem now and then to vignette a quaint picture in stone, and make a rich sombre foreground for the bases of old towers and the resting-places of ancient arches. I suppose its chief architectural triumph, if not the world's finest example of Gothic art, is the Church of St. Pierre, which looks down upon you from its graceful tower as you saunter down the street of St. Jean. A great German writer has pronounced the "renaissance" work at the east end of the building as "the masterpiece of the epoch," while the other extremity of the church is occupied by "the loveliest steeple and tower in the world." Prout has painted it. Pugin used to talk of the majesty of the tall lancet windows of its western façade. To-day it still remains a testimony to the inspiration of the great artists and builders of the past, and a glorious memento of the religious devotion of the founders of Christianity in Europe. The interior is spoiled in an artistic sense, as is the case with many of the Continental churches, by tawdry pictures, wooden candles, ugly confessional boxes, glass chandeliers, and other anachronistic blemishes upon architectural form and beauty. Some of the sculptured pendants of the aisles are very original, and there are legends in stone in the capitals of columns which are not a little curious, notably "Launcelot crossing the sea on his sword," "Aristotle bridled and ridden by the mistress of Alexander," and other reminiscences of ancient fable and romance. But from an historical point of view the most interesting building in Caen is the cathedral church of St. Etienne, or the Abbaye aux Hommes (so called in contradistinction to the Abbaye aux Dames, or La Sainte Trinité, founded by William's wife), where the Norman conqueror of England was buried. A plain marble slab in the chancel marks the spot where his bones once rested. The jealous custodian of the place tells you that a great deal of what was William still lies there. One might quote the grave-digger in *Hamlet* in reply, for the vault is certainly now empty of any human remains of the Conqueror. The Huguenots broke the grave open in 1562 and dispersed the mouldering contents. One thigh-bone alone was preserved and restored to its former resting-place. Why, indeed, " may not imagination trace the noble dust of Alexander, till we find it stopping a bung-hole"? The revolutionists of 1793 felt that it would be eminently consoling to their feelings, and an advantage to their just cause, to disperse that last thigh-bone. They tore open the famous tomb which the Huguenots had violated, and from that day William has indeed become but a memory. There is not even dust enough left of him to stop a bung-hole. He was as unfortunate in his funeral as he was in his proposed long rest. If he conquered when alive, he was a very dead lion indeed when his day was over. His funeral was interrupted by a bystander who claimed the ground, from which, he said, his father had been illegally ejected to build the church. The citizen was backed by his fellows, and the bishop who was conducting the solemn ceremony paid sixty sous to the claimant for the dead monarch's grave space. When the coffin was lowered it struck the side of the vault. The corpse was visible, and it made itself so offensive to the olfactory sense of the crowd that the rites were hurriedly concluded, and Henry, his son, the priests, and the citizens went away, contented with the briefest leave-taking.

VIII.

To those who value the last attentions paid to the dead, William the First's finish will, in a measure, tarnish the so-called "glory" of his life. It is quite clear that the ancient citizens of Caen neither loved nor feared him, otherwise it would not have been permitted that a humble citizen should have challenged him at the grave—he who in war had trampled upon and rended England, and in the days of peace had swept a whole county clean of houses and inhabitants to make a hunting ground near his palace at Winchester. He may, perhaps, have been thought much less of at home than abroad. Normandy proper may have considered his exploits in England of no great account. Agricola, who first circumnavigated this island, and under whose sway the Roman dominion in Britain reached its utmost permanent limit, was not thought much of by the people. They could not understand that there was anything very wonderful about a man who was one of themselves, and presented no special appearance of wisdom and power. Domitian had nevertheless recalled him from Britain because he was jealous of his renown. It is believed that the illustrious Roman was poisoned in consequence. There are many arguments in favour of the happiness and safety of a private station; though, in life, those who are famous will invariably find a wholesome lesson of humility in the comments of their neighbours, or in a visit to their native town or village. Shakespeare was only regarded as an ordinary, pleasant, good-natured gossip at Stratford, even after he had returned to the old town well-to-do and famous. Crabbe, who had won the very heart of the nation by his truthful and touching poems, was surprised to find himself famous in London, for he remarked: "In my own village they think nothing of me." Some people living in the next street could not direct me, a few years ago, to the house where Le Sage was born. The strangers who travel many miles to see the house where Carlyle lived are looked upon as foolish creatures by many of the local inhabitants. In the North, pilgrims in search of the houses occupied by Wordsworth and Southey are regarded by not a few of the natives with pitying glances. The old copy-book philosophy that "familiarity breeds contempt" goes straight to the mark. American presidents would, I suspect, be regarded with much more respect and veneration if it were not for the election campaign, which for the time being brings them down to the practical level of other politicians. No man is a hero to his valet. Lord Palmerston's agricultural neighbours, with whom he chatted about the crops, could never realise that his very name was a great moving power from one end of the world to the other. How many of the inhabitants of St. John's Wood, who used to meet Mrs. Lewes taking a walk with her husband, in Regent's Park, would believe that they were favoured with a sight that thousands of people would have travelled long miles to see. Hardly a group of strangers go to stand by Oliver Goldsmith's tomb outside Temple Church, that loiterers thereabouts do not wonder what they can possibly be looking at. It is a sad reflection that those who live in history have often paid the penalty of melancholy endings. I do not profess to discuss the heroes and heroines of martyrdom, though in Normandy one might be excused for referring to Joan of Arc. Beau Brummell died in a lunatic asylum at Caen, and the secretary and early friend of Napoleon I. breathed his last in the same institution, l'Hospice du Bon Sauveur. It was from Caen that Charlotte Corday set out to assassinate Marat. In the old days the learned Bishop Huet was born here: in modern times Auber, the composer, first saw the light in this quiet, beautiful city, which had also inspired the muse of Clement and Malherbe.

IX.

There is a pretty suburb of Caen, called St. Julien. It is a little world of fine houses, and the district has a history. The territory of St. Julien was originally dependent on the fief of Monsenay, and belonged to Bertrand de Rocheville. He had feudal powers like the Norman knights in England. The inhabitants under the shadow of his castle were his slaves. Indeed, all who went to live in the parish of St. Julien were subject to vassalage. It was, therefore, chiefly occupied by families of people in difficulties, men and women who found freedom less comfortable than vassalage. In the eleventh century the Jews settled down at St. Julien, and carried on the business of usury. It must have been that the money-lenders outside the precincts had agents within. They were at their best in Caen, as a community, no doubt after the slave epoch. In the old days they were under the inspection of a corps of judges exclusively charged with the affairs of the Israelites, and were called the Jews' exchequers. De Bras has an interesting note upon the district: "Where so many fugitives have come to live in order to escape their creditors, are a great many quarries of the whitest stone, soft to work, which on being exposed hardens in such a manner that the injury of the weather, the frost, and the rain cannot harm it." There are not wanting plenty of magnificent testimonials to the truth of the ancient writer's description of Caen stone in many countries. Not far from St. Julien the ancient Leprosy Hospital of the past had its site. It was founded by Henry II., Duke of Normandy and King of England, in 1161, and the historians of the period speak of it as "a wonderful work." There is hardly a darker time to look back upon than during this scourge of leprosy in Europe. Introduced as a consequence of the Crusades, my French "Itinéraire" assures me that Caen was especially smitten. So contagious and revolting was this disease that it was regarded with superstitious awe, which, coupled with the want of therapeutic physic, contributed to its terrible effects. Leprosy was regarded as incurable. The authorities contented themselves with the isolation of the stricken. By degrees, special houses were constructed for them. These came at last to be fixed in distinct localities. There was not a town or village that had not its hospital. In the districts of Douvrer and Cruelly, and also at Mathieu, Villoir, and Lion, they were to be found. The fears which the pest spread gave rise to more than one drama, not less touching in its subject than the story of Xavier de Maistre. When a person was suspected of having taken the disease, he was taken before the local tribunals, who at once ordered an inquiry, and the search and examination of his house. This was effected by a surgeon, often, strange to say, by lepers themselves, with the invariable result that the suspect was thrown into a home of infection, or a veritable hell, condemned to spend there the rest of his miserable days. If the subjects of these hasty investigations were really not lepers when they entered, as must very often have been the case, they soon caught the contagion. The "crime" being thus substantiated, the leper was admitted *à la prébende ou pension du Roi*. The lepers became quite a separate people in the land, with their liberties and their franchises. Struck with civil death, denied the right of willing property or inheriting it, they were allowed temporary use of their possessions during life. The Lazaretto of Henry II., at Caen, was well endowed for the maintenance of all. He instituted in the interests of this hospital the fair of St. Jude, which is still kept up, and is celebrated on the 28th of October. He gave the lepers large gifts and properties. Every three years the town of Caen elected administrators of the Lazaretto, and appointed a chaplain. In the thirteenth century the establishment was directed by a single officer nominated by the King. He was called the Great Lazaretto (*Grand Maladerie*). It is well ascertained that marriage between lepers was allowed, with hideous results. The Lazaretto was occupied three hundred years ago, but in 1696 it was almost deserted, and soon afterwards (the plague having run its terrible course) the institution was converted into a house of correction for beggars. A hundred years afterwards it became a lunatic asylum, and old men in Caen can remember its pauper inmates "stretched out on straw and grovelling in filth, many of them fastened by chains to the damp and noisome walls of their cells." It is only a little more than seventy years ago since the amelioration of their condition was effected. "The good old days," as some of us persist in calling the dark ages, furnish incidents of horror as terrible as any that have been invented or imagined for the punishment of the damned. What a history of misery and death is the story of the world's hospitals for lepers and lunatics, and the condition of European prisons! Reforms of all grievances come sooner or later; but this is no atonement for the sufferings and miseries of delay.

XX.

STRANGE DREAMS.

"The Children of an Idle Brain"—In the Regions of Absurdity—Prophetic of Death—A Reminiscence of the Caskets—Tragedy—Strange Coincidences—What are Dreams?—Problems Solved in Sleep.

I.

WHETHER we regard dreams as "the children of an idle brain, begot of nothing but vain fantasy," or accept them as an important integral part of the human constitution, they offer an interesting field of inquiry. Simply as stray shadows, flitting across the half-sleeping mind, they present an incongruous variety of peculiar incidents—tragic, pathetic, wonderful, ludicrous. Accepted as revelations of a higher state, lost or to come, regarded as the work of certain delicate machinery planted in the human brain by the Divine hand, they assume a certain importance in many authenticated cases of dreams fulfilled. In sleep, with the muscles relaxed, the senses at rest, thought and voluntary motion in repose, the work of the organic functions goes on, the blood circulates, is purified by respiration, and, for the time being (as Dr. Symonds puts it in an excellent little work, to which I am indebted for some of the instances of notable dreams in this bundle of "Cigarette Papers"), the body lives the life of a vegetable. But there are varied degrees of sleep. Some of our senses may be comparatively wakeful whilst others are in sound repose. In this state one organ may receive impressions that will excite activity of association in others that are more or less wakeful. It is this incomplete state of sleep, this semi-repose of the faculties, which produces dreams. Dr. Macnish, "happening to sleep in damp sheets, dreamed he was dragged through a stream." Dr. Symonds witnessed in his sleep what he thought was a prolonged storm of thunder, which he was afterwards able to trace to the light of a candle brought suddenly into the dark room where he had fallen asleep. He relates that a person having a blister applied to his head fancied he was scalped by a party of Indians. I remember, when a boy, sleeping in a strange house, in an old-fashioned room, with an oaken corner-cupboard over the bed. I dreamt that I was being murdered; the assassin struck me on the head, and I awoke with a sense of pain in that region. Putting my hand to my fore-

head I found it sticky—with blood! I felt almost too ill to cry for help, but at length I alarmed the household, and, on procuring a light, it was discovered that a jar of fermented jam had leaked through the bottom of the cupboard and fallen upon my head in a small sluggish stream. A few months ago, shortly

before going to bed, a friend had been discussing with
me the peculiar instincts of animals, and, more particularly, their sense of the coming on of storms.
After this I dreamed I was a Worcestershire shorthorn,
grazing in a pleasant meadow on the Herefordshire
side of the Malvern Hills. I had a number of
companions. Signs of a storm appeared in the sky,
a misty vapour hung on the well-known beacon. I
remember distinctly, although I was a cow, watching,
with a feeling of great delight, the beauty of the
preliminary tokens of the storm. With the other
cows I quietly strolled towards the shelter of an
adjacent tree, and waited until the storm should break
I was chewing the cud, and relished its herbaceous
flavour. I distinctly remember wagging my tail; yet
all the time I had full reasoning faculties, and a lively
sense of the beauties of the scenery.

II.

Dr. Macnish says, once his dreaming travelled so far
into the regions of absurdity that he conceived himself
to be riding upon his own back, one who resem-
blanced himself being mounted on another, and both
animated with a soul appertaining to himself, in such
a manner that he knew not whether he was the carrier
or the carried. These are odd examples of the incongruity of " the imperfection of the dreaming memory,"
which is most strongly illustrated when we dream of

those who are dead. "We believe them still to be living, simply because we have forgotten that they are dead." A friend of Dr. Symonds dreamed that he was dead, and that he carried his own body in a coach to bury it. When he reached the place of burial a stranger said, "I would not advise you, sir, to bury your body in this place, for they are about to build so near it that I have no doubt the body will be disturbed by the builders." "That," replied the dreamer, "is very true; I thank you for the information, and I will remove it to another spot," upon which he awoke.

III.

Of the prophetic character of dreams there are many strangely startling examples. Pepys relates the story "which Luellin did tell me the other day, of his wife upon her deathbed; how she dreamed of her uncle Scobell, and did fortell from some discourse she had with him that she should die four days thence, and no sooner, and did all along say so, and did so." In "Some Passages of the Life and Death of the Right Honourable John, Earl of Rochester, written by his own direction on his deathbed" (1680), his lordship related how Lady Ware's chaplain dreamed he should die the next day, went to bed in apparently perfect health, and died in the morning. In some "Various Examples," given by Mr. Frank Seafield in his excellent work on "The Literature and Curiosities of Dreams," it is related that "My Lady Seymour dreamed that she saw a nest with nine finches in it. And so many children she had by the Earl of

Winchelsey, whose name was Finch." "Anno 1690, one in Ireland dreamed of a brother, or near relation of his, who lived at Amesbury, in Wiltshire, that he saw him riding on the downs, and that two thieves robbed him and murthered him. The dream awakened him; he fell asleep again, and had the like dream.

He wrote to his relation an account of it, and described the thieves' complexion, stature, and clothes, and advised him to take care of himself. Not long after he had received the monitory letter he rode towards Salisbury, and was robbed and murthered; and the murtherers were discovered by his letter and executed." In 1698 Mr. William Smythies, curate of St. Giles's, Cripplegate, published an account of the robbery and murder of John Stockden, victualler, in Grub Street, and the discovery of the murderers by several dreams of Elizabeth, the wife of Thomas Greenwood, a neighbour of the murdered man's. Jung Stilling, in "Theorie der Geister-Kunde," relates that a short time before the Princess Nagotsky, of Warsaw, travelled to Paris (October, 1720), she dreamed that she found herself in a strange apartment, where a man presented a cup to her, and desired her to drink. She declined, and the unknown person said: "You should not refuse; this is the last you will ever drink in your life." In Paris she was taken ill, and the King's physician was sent to her. On his arrival the Princess showed great signs of astonishment; asked the reason, she said: "You perfectly resemble the man whom I saw in a dream at Warsaw; but I shall not die this time, for this is not the same apartment which I saw in my dream." She recovered, and eventually, in good health, forgot her dream and the fears it had created. Upwards of a year afterwards, however, she was dissatisfied with her lodgings at the hotel, and requested to have apartments prepared for her in a convent at Paris. Immediately on entering the room she exclaimed: "It is all over with me. I shall not leave this room alive; it is the one I saw in my dream at Warsaw." She died soon afterwards, in the same apartment, of an ulcer in the throat, occasioned by the drawing of a tooth.

IV.

In the *Gentleman's Magazine* for December, 1787, there is a wonderful account of the discovery of a murder through a dream. The narrative called forth a note from A. J., who said that some few years before the erection of the well-known lighthouses called the Caskets, an islander dreamed that a ship had been wrecked, and that some part of the crew had saved themselves upon the rocks. He told this story the next morning on the quay; but the sailors, despite their superstitious characteristics, treated it as an idle dream. The next night he dreamed the same thing, and prevailing upon a companion to go out with him the next morning to the spot, in a boat, they found three poor wretches there, and brought them ashore.

V.

Dr. Abercrombie says he is enabled to give the following anecdote as entirely authentic:—A lady dreamed that an aged female relative had been murdered by a black servant, and the dream occurred more than once. She was then so strangely impressed by it that she went to the house of the lady to whom it related, and prevailed upon a gentleman to watch in an adjoining room the following night. About three o'clock in the morning the gentleman, hearing footsteps on the stairs, left his place of concealment, and met the servant carrying up a quantity of coals. Being questioned as to where he was going, he replied, in a confused manner, that he was going to mend his mistress's fire, which, at three o'clock in the morning, in the middle of summer, was evidently impossible; and, on further investigation, a strong knife was found beneath the coals. "Another lady," he says, "dreamed that a boy, her nephew, had been drowned along with some companions with whom he had been engaged to go on a sailing excursion in the Firth of Forth. She sent for him in the morning, and prevailed on him to give up his engagement. His companions went and were all drowned." The alarm with regard to the disappearance of Maria Martin was brought to its height by the mother dreaming, on three successive nights, that her daughter had been murdered, and buried in the Red Barn. Upon this, search was made, the floor taken up, and the murdered body discovered. The story is fully related in *Chambers's Journal* for October, 1832.

V.

In a note to Dr. Binns's "Anatomy of Sleep," Lord Stanhope is credited with relating that a Lord of the Admiralty, who was on a visit to Mount Edgecumbe, dreamed that, walking on the sea-shore, he picked up a book which appeared to be the log of a ship of war of which his brother was captain. He opened it, and read an entry of the latitude, longitude, as well as the day and hour, to which was added, "Our captain died." The company endeavoured to comfort him by laying a wager that the dream would be falsified, and a memorandum was made in writing of what he had stated, which was afterwards confirmed in every particular. J. Noel Paton relates the extraordinary fulfilment of a dream of his mother's involving the death of a dearly beloved sister. The murder of Mr. Perceval, which was seen in a vision more than one hundred and fifty miles from the spot where it occurred, is a well-known story, and authentic. A lady friend of mine vouches for the truth of the following story:—"My mother resided in London, and one of her children was sent out to nurse. She dreamed soon after that she went to the nurse's house, and saw her own child, looking half-starved, and faintly struggling for a crust of bread which the nurse's child was eating. The children were both in one cradle. My mother went the very next day, and found the children exactly as she saw them, her own child weak, ill, and hungry." Of a member of my own family, it is related that he added, with some difficulty, two keys to a musical wind instrument. He had prepared the drawings, and the new instrument was about to be manufactured, when he dreamed that a military band passed through the city where he resided, the leader of which used an instrument with the very additional keys that he had invented. The next day a regiment *en route* for London did pass through the town, and the leader was playing upon such an instrument, the first manufacture of a firm which had just brought out the new bugle.

VII.

Mr. John Hill Burton, in his work, "Narratives from Criminal Trials in Scotland," urges that no ghost-story, or story of dream-coincidences, could stand the sifting examination of a court of justice. Dr. Symonds evidently entertains a similar opinion, though he gives us what would seem some startling evidence leading to a contrary conviction. Before any such cases are received as true occurrences, he very properly asks that they shall undergo most rigorously all the tests of evidence. Regarding them as instances of a kind of revelation, he says:—" We look for a final cause; but we discern none, unless it be the possibility of some influence on the spiritual condition of the individuals." "Ay, there's the rub." A writer in *Blackwood* puts the question, but does not answer it: "Are appearances in dreams imaginary visions; or are they, however inexplicable the mode, the actual spirit-presence of the persons whose image they bear?" It is not my intention to discuss this point, which may be left to the philosophers, medical and scientific. My purpose is simply to compile for the reader a few notable instances of dreaming, curious as records of "dream-life," and suggestive for thoughtful inquiry.

VIII.

Whether, by some extraordinary action of the spiritual essence, warnings of disaster or prophetic monition may be communicated to the brain through the mystic medium of a dream; or whether our fancies of the night are the mere mixed associations of time and place and memory wrought into apparent reasonable shape by accidental circumstances,—these are questions that may hardly be fully answered. It cannot be doubted that this exercise of the faculties when in a semi-state of rest is for our benefit in some way; and, whatever may be said to the contrary, the evidence in favour of the extraordinary fulfilment of dreams, altogether beyond human explanation, is too strong for disbelief. That dreams are to be catalogued and interpreted as the believers in "Oneirocriticon" set forth is simply nonsense; but they often serve important ends, and seeing how great a portion of our lives is occupied with sleep, to dream is to fill up a great blank with sensations of pleasure, hope, joy, that last often long after the dream is over, tending to an elevation of the aspirations and ambition of the dreamer. There are mathematicians who have solved great problems in dreams. Franklin frequently formed correct opinions of important matters in dreams; the mind has been inspired with beautiful poems in sleep, Coleridge's "Kublah Khan" for example, though this may, perhaps, hardly be spoken of in the sense of what is called an ordinary healthy dream, seeing that it may probably have been greatly influenced by opium. And now—

> "To all, to each, a fair good-night,
> And pleasing dreams, and slumbers light."

XXI.

COMING INTO MONEY.

The Slot of Fortune—Fox's One Bet—The Poor Man and his £20,000—What it feels like to come into a Fortune—Sydney Smith and his Yorkshire Living—Coming Events.

1.

IN the once popular farce of "The Lottery Ticket" fortune smiles upon a poor but honest person. As a rule on the principle that money is attracted by money, and good fortune by its like, lottery prizes and the winning horses in Derby sweepstakes go to men and women who could do very well without any addition whatever to their banking account. They have no need of windfalls, though it is natural enough that, dropping their coin into the automatic slot of fortune, they should hope for the winning prize; but, after the passing sensation of depositing their little investment, they give the matter no further thought.

"When a City acquaintance comes to me," said a friend of mine the other day, "suggesting a good thing, I look into it for a few minutes, trust his word, hand him the necessary few hundred pounds, and think no more of it. If the subject does occur to me, I simply say to myself, 'All right, my few hundreds are gone; there's an end of it.' If it turns up trumps, and the few hundreds bring themselves back with a few to keep them company, all well and good; but that is my idea of speculation."

One can easily understand, on the other side, with what great hopes the poor man drops his penny into fortune's slot and insinuates his hand into the lucky bag. My own experience of that annual gamble, the Derby sweep, in connection with a notable club, is entirely in accordance with the proverb that "money attracts money."

II.

"My own experience also," said Fox. "I never bet. I would not be so unjust to a popular horse as to handicap him with my ill-luck. When I say I never bet, I mean as a rule. I did once, some fourteen or sixteen years ago. I knew a remarkable racing authority, who watched racing with the keen interest of the student, and the disinterestedness of a sporting gentleman, who himself never bet more than half-a-crown in his life. But he loved horses almost as much as Mr. Gulliver after his eventful residence among the Houyhnhnm. Over a glass of his old port the day before the Derby of that year was run, I obtained his forecast of the race on the merits of the horses, and, in a sportive way, next morning made a bet with a professional gentleman belonging to a professional sporting club, in which I backed myself to name the first three horses. It was what the gentleman who took it called a very sporting investment, and he gave me long odds. My surprise was probably greater than his when on the next evening, thinking little or nothing of my bet, I took up an evening paper and saw the Derby numbers, giving my three horses, 1, 2, 3. I had won a hundred pounds. I was astonished the next day to receive a wire from the gentleman who had lost, asking me to give him a few days' grace, congratulating me on my success, and hoping I had made other bets in the same direction. To cut a long story short, my betting merchant came to grief, went through the Bankruptcy Court for other debts, and generally 'played out.' That was almost the only bet I ever made, and you see my luck was not sufficiently emphatic to hold on up to settlement. But how have we drifted into this subject of fortune?"

III.

"Because," I replied, "of the splendid exception to the rule we were discussing which has recently taken place in France. The owner of the winning number in the French Exhibition Lottery is a poor man; not only poor, but a good fellow, a worthy husband, and the father of a large family. Furthermore, he is interesting to me from the fact that he is a printer; if he had been a journalist out and out I could not have felt a greater satisfaction in his good fortune. When you come to think of it, a millionaire might have won the prize—a Rothschild, a great financier, a man to whom twenty thousand pounds would be as a fiver to you or me. Think of it; twenty thousand pounds for this poor printer! He only bought one ticket in the Lottery; its number was 54,639. He is a Belgian by birth, but a naturalised Frenchman; and, in addition to his wife and six children, has an aged mother dependent upon him for support. Interviewed by Parisian journalists, he tells them that his life has been one of hard work and that he has seen much misery, but in future he hopes to 'live on his income,' like a gentleman. An English newspaper moralist, I see, while inclined to be congratulatory upon the fact that for once in a way a great prize has fallen to a poor man, is disposed to question whether he will be any happier for this piece of great luck. Whether suddenly acquired wealth always means greater happiness in life is a question which he seems very much to doubt; and yet I suspect he would himself take the most extravagant risks of misery with an endowment of twenty thousand pounds. It is difficult to imagine the feelings of the poor man coming so unexpectedly into a great fortune."

IV.

"Oh, I don't know," remarked Fox, "I should imagine they were very much like the sensation one feels on achieving some big success. I have known the time when I have felt inclined to shout and scream with delight, after months, in one case years, of patient investigation, coming straight upon the clue and finally laying my hand upon the man himself. Indeed, I question if your intellectual labourer in literature and art, who wakes up some morning to find himself famous, does not enjoy a far keener sense of happiness than can enter into the wildest dreams of your printer friend with his lucky lottery ticket."

"You think it requires the nervous touch of intellectual sensibility to feel keenly about anything?"

"I do," said Fox.

"And yet," I replied, "I am not sure that anything can for the moment cap the intensity of the pleasure with which a starving man suddenly finds himself invited to a good square meal. One night I was accosted in the Strand by a man who said he was hungry. He looked half-starved. It was a bitterly cold night. His clothes were thin. They were not the attire of ordinary beggary; nor were they the cleanly brushed threadbare garments of the genteel mendicant. I questioned the man. He told me the truth. Drink had brought him to ruin. And he too was a printer. For a week he had not drunk a drop of alcohol; for two days he had eaten nothing but a crust. Nobody would employ him; and if they would he was in such a trembling condition that he could not pick up type, or adjust a line when he had picked it up. No, he did not want money just then, but food; he should pull himself together by-and-by; he would rather commit suicide than apply for parish relief, and rather die than steal. He walked by my side; we came to a hot sausage shop. The food was smoking; the savoury odours of the kitchen permeated the street in front of the shop. 'Come in here,' I said. He followed me. 'Give this man six sausages, two pieces of bread, and a pint of ale, at once, please.' I paid the little score, and the food was promptly placed before the starving printer. He did not speak; he looked too dazed to thank me; but I watched him from the outside of the shop. Didn't he enjoy himself! His fellow-printer of Paris could not have been more delighted when he got news of his good luck. The scene recalled to my mind the Americanism of the fellow who said he had 'got a thirst on him' that he would 'not sell for fifty dollars.' After all physical enjoyment is the keenest."

"And the most evanescent," said Fox; "though, no doubt, to be warmed when you are cold, to drink when you are thirsty, to eat when you are hungry, is the highest happiness as long as it lasts."

v.

"To come into possession of anything, even of moderate value, but unexpectedly, has a very stirring influence. That is why the old surprise party, which obtained many years ago in England, and which has been introduced with other good English things into America, was always a pleasure. The proprietor of a popular newspaper described to me the other day the delight a gentleman in one of the great Civil Service departments of the Government experienced in winning a Prize Organ. Moreover, he was the hero of the office for the day; was introduced to new people as the gentleman who had won the great guessing prize. Anything which distinguishes a man from the crowd is more or less gratifying to the man in question, but when in addition it puts money in his purse, or an organ into his drawing-room, without any expense to himself, even the merest trifle, the enjoyment is all the keener. What would not the Reverend and witty Sydney Smith have given for a lucky lottery ticket, with twenty thousand pounds behind it, when he was transported to his Yorkshire living, where there had not been a resident parson for one hundred and fifty years?"

VI.

"He went down to Yorkshire, fresh from London, not knowing a turnip from a carrot, and without capital to complete the conditions of his preferment. There is something almost as pathetic as it is humorous in his rural struggles. Having tried to effect an exchange, you remember, and failed, he obtained from his friend, the Archbishop, a year's time to build his house; whereupon he set his shoulder to the wheel, and sent for an architect, who produced plans which would have ruined him. 'You build for glory, sir— I for use,' said Sydney Smith, returning him his plans with five-and-twenty pounds; and then proceeded to concoct a plan for producing his parsonage house. You don't remember these particular passages in the witty Dean's Memoirs?"

"No," said Fox.

"Apropos," I continued, "of what many good men could do with twenty thousand pounds—and,

SYDNEY SMITH'S NEIGHBOURS.

indeed, with nineteen thousand less than twenty—the situation of Sydney Smith, for more reasons than one, is worth glancing at. He was advised to make his own bricks of his own clay; did so; when the kiln was opened, the bricks were no good; went forth on his solitary horse; brought bricks and timber. Was advised by a neighbouring gentleman to employ oxen; bought four; they took to fainting—required buckets of sal volatile to keep them up. Did then what he ought to have done at first—took the advice of a farmer; sold his oxen; bought horses. Finally built his house; landed his family there, in spite of frost and wet. Was warned and remonstrated with—he and his belongings might as well commit suicide as enter upon a house so newly built. Nevertheless, nine months after laying his first stone, in went his family, and he performed his promise to the Archbishop to the letter, by issuing forth at midnight to meet the last cart—to meet the cook and the cat—which had stuck in the mud, to fairly establish them before midnight; the feat—taking ignorance, inexperience, and poverty into consideration—requiring no small amount of energy. 'It made me a poor man for many years,' he says, 'but I never repented it. I turned schoolmaster, to educate my son.' Mrs. Sydney turned schoolmistress, to educate his girls. He turned farmer because he could not let his land, and he had other difficulties too numerous to mention.

Possessing little furniture, he bought a cartload of deals, took into his service a carpenter who came to him for parish relief with a face like a full moon, established him in a barn, and furnished his house. And so the story goes on; and I do not know in the range of autobiography anything more human or instructive, cynic as the reverend gentleman undoubtedly was, but with a firm underlying stratum of human nature and common-sense."

VII.

"Yes," said Fox, "what a glorious thing a winning lottery ticket would have been to such a man! But supposing he had possessed it, what about his Memoirs? He would not have had to build that house; therefore he would not have had to relate these interesting human experiences, which, both to him and to his readers, would in after years be so entertaining, instructive, and, as you say, delightful. The truth is, we never know what is best for us. Twenty thousand pounds may, as your newspaper friend suggests, be a bad thing for your French printer."

"A good deal depends upon his wife," I remarked. "He is reported to be, as the newspapers put it, a good husband, with a family and an aged mother to support. As a rule, the good husband is made by the good wife; the good wife, as a rule, is a sensible clever woman. Without a clever and devoted wife no French or any other printer could bring up half-a-dozen children, and support an aged mother."

"Then here's to the clever and devoted wife," said Fox in his happiest mood, "and long life and happiness to the lucky French printer!"

XXII.

"A QUIET PIPE."

Spurgeon and Carlyle on Tobacco—"Smoke and Poesy"—"A Cigarette-maker's Romance" — "Cope's Smoke-room Booklets"—A Whistlerian Inspiration—A Flower from "The Smoker's Garland"—James Thompson, the Poet—Tarass Bulba Schmidt.

YOU have been hard hit; a professed friend has gone

LAMB AND COLERIDGE.

back on you. A quiet pipe. The stock which you

purchased under the belief that it would go to a premium has gone down to zero. A quiet pipe. You have struck a streak of ill-luck generally. A quiet pipe. The horizon of your worldly prospects has grown dark with threat of storm and tempest. A quiet pipe. Presently there is a change for the better; the sun shines; your new book is a great success; you have paid off that mortgage; the wife of your bosom shall have those diamond earrings; your next summer holiday shall be long and luxurious. All the same, a quiet pipe.

In joy or sorrow, for all seasons, in every clime, under all circumstances, a quiet pipe is a most true and sweet companion. There is a certain intolerance in the theology of the Apostle Spurgeon which I dislike; but he has the courage of his convictions, and standing up in his great pulpit he thanked God for tobacco. What a comfort the generous weed must have been to him in his trying days of illness, and in his weary advance towards convalescence! Carlyle knew the blessings of a quiet pipe. When, invalided, and submitting himself to Dr. Franks at Cannes, he said, " I'll do anything, doctor, ye tell me, but ye manna stop my pipe."

II.

" I image to myself the little smoky room at *The Salutation and Cat*," wrote Lamb to Coleridge, " where we have sat together through winter nights, beguiling the cares of life with Poesy." On another occasion he asks his friend, " When shall we two smoke again ? Last night I had been in a sad quandary of spirits, in what they call the evening ; but a pipe and some generous port, and King Lear (being alone) had their effects as solacers." King Lear and a pipe ! It surely needed the good red wine to keep back Elia's tears over the woes of the heart-broken king ! But a sympathetic soul finds a certain melancholy pleasure in sharing another's woes ; and Lamb was endowed with that capacity for love and friendship that makes a man's pleasures as keen as his sorrows. One can easily imagine him poring over the sad story of *King Lear* (being alone, as he says), and needing all the solace of his good pipe to moderate his grief. He knew what sorrow was : and he was acquainted with grief. And yet what a merry, pleasant, joyful companion he could be—and was. How merry, how happy, how human, you—to whom Elia is a familiar figure—know well enough : and you to whom he is still a stranger, cannot do better than make his acquaintance through the medium of one of the daintiest little volumes of a growing library of the literature of tobacco, from which the accompanying illustration (together with the other pictorial adornments of this bundle of " Cigarette Papers," not to mention the frontispiece that gives its title) is reproduced—the picture of Lamb and Coleridge smoking together in that self-same tavern of the *Salutation and Cat*, mentioned in his epistolary reference to winter nights of chat and sweet discourse: winter nights which he had afterwards recalled over many a quiet pipe. I suppose there is no greater aid to reflection, no better stimulus to reverie, than a pipe. When I say a pipe I do not, of course exclude a cigar or a cigarette. I take pipe as a generic term for a smoke, as the Americans make rum apply to every kind of spirit that men drink. To some the solace of a pipe is deeper than the content that belongs to a fine cigar; but there are many who find a swift sensuous pleasure in a cigarette that neither pipe nor cigar can supply. Have you read Marion Crawford's "A Cigarette-maker's Romance"? How the aroma of the factory and the dust of the desiccated leaf fill the pleasant atmosphere which envelopes the Count and his devoted little worshipper and friend. If you want a picture of the engrossing and absorbing influence of a cigarette smoked in a good cause, treated as a friend, caressed as a sympathiser, burned with the affection that I never dare hope any cigarette of my making will inspire, turn to Crawford's second chapter and contemplate the hero and heroine of his calm and gentle romance. "Vjera was silent, but she softly withdrew her hand from his and gazed at the people in the distance. The Count smoked without speaking for several minutes, closing his eyes as though revolving a great problem in his mind, then glancing sidelong at his companion's face, hesitating as though about to speak, checking himself and shutting his eyes again in meditation. Holding his cigarette between his teeth, he clasped his fingers together tightly, unclasped them again, and let his arms fall on each side of him." And then suddenly came his decision; he had formed it with the fragrant breath of the cigarette on his lips; with the help and encouragement of the soothing weed: and be sure the decision was worthy of him and the occasion.

III.

But it was of Lamb we were chatting. I have him before me, pipe in hand, half enveloped in wreaths of genial smoke. He decorates the title-page of one of the first volumes of the dainty library I just now mentioned—it is called "Cope's Smoke-room Booklets"; and I don't know when I have passed a more delightful hour than they have afforded me, not forgetting their promise of charming hours to come. They are not only devoted to the ethics of smoking, they do not simply take account of the history of tobacco and the joy thereof: they are biographies of famous smokers—chats with sages—and they are full of recollections of such song and poesy as have found their inspiration in the golden weed of the sunny lands. I have rolled a quiet cigar over "Smokiana," recently issued by the famous bibliopole and publisher Quarritch. It is a delightful souvenir of pipe and tobacco; but its cover is not half as dainty and artistic as the wrappers that enfold the compilations and original treatises of "Cope's Smoke-room Booklets." I am inclined to think the decorative binding of these present "Cigarette Papers" showy, not to say taking, but "The Smoker's Text Book," "The Smoker's Garland," "Charles Lamb," "Thomas Carlyle," and the other *brochures* issued up to date from the office of *Cope's Tobacco Plant*, are far in advance of my publisher's presentation of these light and miscellaneous notes, artistic though it be with its design of fluttering papers that fancy may fill and smoke. Studies in grey and black, in red and gold, with smoky suggestions of ashy browns, the Cope covers might satisfy even Whistler himself, and give a thrill of joy to our Oscar Wilde, who could not fail to approve the definite lines, the sharp firm titles, and symbolic vignettes—sharp and firm enough for the sternest opponent of the impressionist school—a rare combination of realism and fancy.

IV.

I think it was Whistler who first made his bow as pamphleteer in covers of simple brown paper. The effect was not altogether pleasant. The Christmas Card people followed suit, and made brown paper typical of "hard times," but Copes have lifted brown paper into a place of honour and distinction. Thomas Carlyle silhouetted against a flat gold panel, amidst graded tones of brown, is worthy of a frame, and the table-talk of the book itself is selected and compiled with rare judgment. There is nothing very comforting in Carlyle's sayings, but now and then you come upon one, such as "The wealth of man is the number of things which

he loves and blesses, which he is loved and blessed by!"

What a smoker he was! And how he loved

his pipe! "The government," he said, "lay a tax of some hundreds per cent. upon the poor man's pipe, while the rich man's wine pays scarcely one-tenth of this impost ; but it is a comfort to think that (as I have been told) the amount of Tobacco smuggled is about as great as that which pays the duty." Regarding tobacco as a necessity, he hated to have it made costly. "The smuggler," he said, "is the Lord Almighty of the Chancellor of the Exchequer, saying to him, 'Thus far shalt thou go and no further.'" Loving silence and meditation, Carlyle naturally loved tobacco, and he loved it in one way— tucked into a long clay pipe. "Nobody comes whose talk is half so good to me as silence. I fly out of the way of everybody, and would much rather smoke a pipe of wholesome tobacco than talk to any one in London just now." What must the intolerant anti-smoker think of such a declaration as this? "Tobacco is one of the divinest benefits that has ever come to the human race." And how catholic it is! Smokers are of no party. Lord Tennyson enjoys a pipe ; Mr. Labouchere a cigarette : Bret Harte smokes almost as many cigars in a year as Mark Twain, and Henry Irving often hurries over his dinner for the sake of the cigar that follows it. One might fill a volume of modern instances of famous men who smoke.

But if you would have ample excuse for smoking, turn over the leaves of "The Smoker's Text Book"

THOMAS CARLYLE.

and "The Smoker's Garland." They will approve your pipe, endorse your cigar, and commend your cigarette with maxims in prose and verse, and in such sweet and soothing measure that you may be sure they have been written under the dreamy influence of the weed, and collected together over many a reflective pipe. There is an apostrophe to "My Cigarette" from the *Harvard College Crimson*, which I cannot refrain from including in this special bundle, inscribed "A Quiet Pipe"—there is something so fresh and winning in both words and metre:—

"My cigarette! The amulet
  That charms afar unrest and sorrow;
The magic wand that, far beyond
  To-day, can conjure up to-morrow—
Like love's desire, thy crown of fire
  So softly with the twilight blending,
And, ah! meseems a poet's dreams
  Are in thy wreaths of smoke ascending.

"My cigarette! Can I forget
  How Kate and I, in sunny weather,
Sat in the shade the elm trees made,
  And rolled the fragrant weed together?
I, at her side, beatified
  To hold and guide her fingers willing;
She, rolling slow the paper's snow,
  Putting my heart in with the filling!

"My cigarette! I see her yet—
  The white smoke from her red lips curling,
Her dreaming eyes, her soft replies,
  Her gentle sighs, and laughter purling!

> Ah! dainty roll, whose parting soul
>   Ebbs out in many a snowy billow,
> I, too, would burn, if I might earn
>   Upon her lips so sweet a pillow.
>
> "Ah, cigarette! The gay coquette
>   Has long forgot the flames she lighted,
> And you and I unthinking by
>   Alike are thrown, alike are slighted.
> The darkness gathers fast without,
>   A raindrop on my window plashes;
> My cigarette and heart are out,
>   And nought is left me but their ashes!"

I think Lamb might have applauded these lines. Carlyle would probably have passed them by with some stinging epigram about fools. Smokers glory in having Carlyle on their side, but they love their champion Lamb. You taste the flavour of the fragrant weed in his work, and you are grateful to Providence that provided him with this antidote to his sorrows.

V.

Lamb's slight stammer must have given point to many of his witticisms both in the way of attack and repartee. He reminds me of a New York gentleman named Gilmore, who is celebrated as a wit. He has the Lamb stutter. One day a lady met him in Boston, and was delighted to find, as she believed, that Gilmore was getting the better of his affliction. "Why, Mr.

Gilmore, you do not stammer so much here in Boston as when I met you in New York!" "N—no," said Gilmore, "N—new Y—york's a bigger c—city!"

As a set-off to the lighter booklets of the series, there is a volume of selections from James Thompson's original contributions to *Cope's Tobacco Plant*. Mr. Thompson had a chequered career as an army teacher, clerk, shorthand writer, journalist, author. His story is told in a well-written and interesting biography by Mr. H. S. Salt, recently published. At one time he was Mr. Bradlaugh's secretary, and later filled positions in connection with several public companies. For several years before he died he devoted himself exclusively to literary work. It was not until 1880 that his first volume was published, chiefly through the disinterested kindness of Mr. Bertram Dobell. This book was "The City of Dreadful Night, and other Poems." The title-poem had already, on its first publication in the *National Reformer*, attracted the attention of eminent persons, including George Meredith and George Eliot, and received especial notice from the *Academy* and the *Spectator*. Then followed "Vane's Story, Weddah and Om-el-Bonain, and other Poems," during the same year, and in 1881 a volume of prose called "Essays and Phantasies," both of which were well received. Recognition came too late, for Thompson died in the following year. Since his death two other volumes,

JAMES THOMPSON,
Author of "The City of Dreadful Night."

one of verse and one of prose, have been issued—namely, "A Voice from the Nile, and other Poems," with Mr. Dobell's memoir, and "Satires and Profanities," with an introductory note by Mr. Foote. Both books are dated 1884. The volume of selections under notice is a tribute to the scholarly flavour of the *Tobacco Plant* (to which, from 1875, he had been a salaried contributor), whose pages are none the less instructive and entertaining that they come out amidst the throb and beat of the factory in Lord Nelson Street, with the aroma of the Virginian leaf, and not from a London printing machine, wet and clammy with the mist and fog of Fleet Street.

It seems to me to be a most pleasant and commendable thing to have a great manufacturing firm busy with the literature of its special product, and availing itself of the best art, and the most graphic pens and pencils, in the work of its exploitation. Many years ago I spent some hours in a great English factory, chiefly devoted to the production of cigarettes. When the work-bell rang in *Carmen* my memory always adapted the scene to the opera. As I sat down to add this new bundle to these "Cigarette Papers," I was interrupted by the arrival of Marion Crawford's "A Cigarette-maker's Romance," and the workshop of Christian Fischelowitz has added a new but kindred picture to the others, and next to the Count and Vjera I find intense satisfaction in Tarass

Bulba Schmidt. He was the chief cutter in the little Munich factory. Here is a picture of him. "On the present occasion, having sliced through an unusually long package of leaves, and having encountered an exceptional number of obstacles in doing so, he thought fit to pause, draw a long breath, wipe the perspiration from his sullen forehead with a pocket-handkerchief in which the neutral tints predominated. This operation, preparatory to a rest of ten minutes, having been successfully accomplished, Tarass Schmidt picked up a tiny oblong bit of paper which had found its way to his feet from one of the girls' tables, took a pinch of the freshly cut tobacco beside him, and rolled a cigarette in his palm with one hand, while he felt in his pocket for a match with the other. Then, in the midst of a great cloud of fragrant smoke, he sat down upon the edge of his cutting block and looked at his companions. After a few moments of deep thought he gave expression to his meditations." My meditations, for the moment, are at an end. I will retire in the midst of Schmidt's fragrant cloud, and leave you also, my friends, to your own meditations over "a quiet pipe."

XXIII.

"SHE WAS A BEAUTIFUL WOMAN."

Fox and an Interesting Prisoner—Snobs and "Local Lords"—"The Wild West"—A Lady of Birth and Wealth—A Photograph—She calls!—Wants to be an Actress and start a Paper—She tells her Story—I introduce her to a Great Lawyer—Suspected, Denounced; Prosperous and Scornful nevertheless—During the Merry Days of a Prosperous Season—Fox speaks again.

MR. FOX.

I.

"I HAVE just been visiting a certain prison," said Fox, "where that lady with the various aliases and many adventures is confined, 'a Scotch lassie, ye ken,' for letting in tradesmen at the West End, and committing other swindling depredations."

"Once she was a certain Miss B.," I suggest, using Fox's cautious phraseology.

"Yes, the same," he said, with a snap of his thin lips, "a pretty, clever, and most audacious woman."

"True; and somehow I don't think I pitied certain persons who fell into her trap, caught by her pair of ponies, her references to her aristocratic connections, and other appeals to the natural snobbism of our nature."

"But that is how nearly all dupes fall before the swindler's wiles, be the swindler man or woman," remarks Fox; "the average Britisher—Heaven bless him!—is not to be done by Mr. Smith or Mr. Brown, but he falls an easy victim to Lord Brownesworth, or the Viscount Smythson. Is it not so?"

"Sometimes, no doubt."

"Sometimes!" said Fox, with his cynical smile, "always; for a liberty-loving free country, our fellow-citizens, my dear sir, are the most arrant snobs; and in the rural districts, your local lord and your county lady literally walk over the non-titled people, and the shop-keepers in the little towns grovel at their feet. Why, madame, whom I have just seen serving her time at oakum, and other lively occupations, mashed all the men she met in business; her sealskin jacket, her ponies, her dogs, and her brag—the illegitimate daughter of a duke, who allowed her five thousand a year; then the wife of a wealthy admiral or general; then the lady bountiful of a poor district; then the philanthropist of a colony: why, my dear friend, she was whatever she pleased to be!"

"And how did she look when you saw her in gaol the other day?" I asked.

"Splendid, splendid!" said Fox, rubbing his hands, "her big eyes as defiant as ever, her complexion a little paler than usual, her figure lithe, and her manner a pleasant condescension—a deuced clever woman, sir: and when she comes out she will start afresh, and get back again, depend upon it, into luxurious quarters; not an immoral woman in the very bad sense, but a swindler at heart, a pirate, a female corsair."

"By the way, they hung one of that kind of women in the western wilds of America, the other day, did you see?"

"No," said Fox, with a smile, as much as to say what he had not seen or heard was hardly worth attention; but I insisted upon telling him how "the queen of the horse stealers," with her male companion, had been executed by a vigilance committee, which Fox thought a barbarous business. Fox likes a proper trial, and everything regular in the way of justice. But to return to his prison heroine, I said, "My dear Fox, I knew the lady."

"Knew her!" he exclaimed.

"Yes," I said, "I would have imagined that you had seen the account of my adventure with her, which I related long before her arrest, in an assumed name so far as she was concerned, but with my own signature."

"Never heard of it," said Fox.

"Well," I replied, "as the lady will shortly have fulfilled her term of imprisonment, the story may be considered quite *à-propos*; and if you will sit quietly and smoke your cigar in peace, I will give you the benefit of my curious experience."

II.

She was a beautiful woman. How I came to know her was in this way:—

One morning I received from a correspondent in Scotland an exciting account of a dashing feat of horsemanship performed by a lady of rare courage and feminine loveliness. The story appeared in one of the journals, and my friend followed it up by sending me cabinet portraits of the heroine. The sun-painter rarely flatters, except under the manipulation of Van der Weyde, Mayall, or Sarony. The portraits displayed the charms of a lovely and aristocratic-looking young woman. My friend had not known her long, but he was evidently in love with her. He informed me that she was a lady of birth and wealth, and that she was going to give her family umbrage by entering upon a course of professional study for the stage. She had already signified her intention of removing to London, and as she was an orphan and of age, no one had any control over her. She would call upon me for advice, and he hoped I would do all I could for

18

her. I was under some obligation of courtesy to my Scotch friend, and I assured him that the lady should not lack good advice, and any useful introductions I could give her.

III.

In due course her ladyship called. She was all my correspondent's fancy had painted her. Tall, a dainty figure, with sparkling eyes, and a healthy complexion. Miss Ogilvie Westerne spoke with a slight Scotch accent, that added an additional charm to a musical voice. She was splendidly dressed, and she was evidently quite innocent of London life. She was very angry with my correspondent for sending her portrait to me. It seemed to her a liberty, and I gathered at once from her blushes and confusion that she knew how much the poor man loved her. I gave her some useful advice, and she called upon me again, giving me to understand on this second visit that she did not like Mr. John Ryder's tutorship; he was too severe for her, though he was a good elocutionist. She thought she should place herself in the professional hands of Mr. Hermann Vezin. "I have not come to London to act," she said; "I have been in the

HERMANN VEZIN.

habit of writing for the press. I have a diploma as a practitioner in one of the Scotch hospitals; I have studied politics; I have written a play; and so you see I have a good many irons in the fire. What I want to do first is to buy a newspaper."

"Have you a large fortune?" I asked.

"Yes," she replied, smiling.

"Then you had better have a theatre as well as a newspaper," I said, "if you are anxious to get your troubles over quickly."

"You think you are talking to the inexperienced girl described by your Edinburgh correspondent," she said. "Let me undeceive you; I have been my own mistress almost since I was a child, and have had a long career of work: I have invested money in many strange ventures and never lost any; I am lucky, and when you talk sarcastically of my having a theatre, you don't dream that before six months are over my head I *shall* have a newspaper *and* a theatre; I can afford it."

IV.

I was amused to see this girlish-looking enthusiast take the press and the drama by their respective collars in this way; but her downright earnestness and enthusiasm compelled my respect.

"You have agents or solicitors, Miss Westerne?" I asked.

276 "CIGARETTE PAPERS."

MISS OGILVIE WESTERNE.

"Of course; oh yes," she said.

"Then ask their advice before you embark upon these speculations."

"No, no; I never ask their advice; I simply tell them what I wish. I want *you* to advise me, and, if you will let me know of any good newspaper in the market for sale, I will buy it. And though I would not hurt your feelings for the world, I shall ask you to make it a business matter between us."

"Pardon me," I said, "I will be no party to an enterprise that cannot fail to be a source of serious anxiety to a lady whom I am asked to help with my advice. Can you guess how much money has been invested in the little journal, in the office of which you are now sitting?"

"I have not the least idea," she replied.

"Twenty thousand pounds," I said.

She was not frightened.

"And I would sell it for a couple of thousand this moment—but not to you, not to you."

She only smiled and said I was very frank and matter-of-fact, but she begged me to understand that her financial resources were sufficient to warrant her in buying a newspaper and taking a theatre. First, however, she must have a very clever business man and secretary. She looked at me with a fascinating glance, and I confess I began to admire the brave, daring Scotch beauty.

V.

A week had elapsed before she called again. She had taken rooms in a house where the people had not treated her quite properly. The proprietor had evidently tried to gain some undue influence over her by prying into her affairs.

"The truth is, my dear sir, I had better tell you who I am, and then you will advise me with confidence, and I shall return your own candour with an honesty that I am sure you will respect. I am the illegitimate daughter of the Earl of ———. I have an estate in Scotland, and a considerable income, which is paid to me quarterly by the Earl's agents. I am extravagant. I have always been accustomed to buy everything I like, and this person has found that I owe some debts in the North, and he has been making inquiries about me, and opening my letters. The accounts are only a few hundred pounds, and my agents will pay them, but the quarter is not up; and don't you think it is a very shameful thing for this man to try and get money out of me—I have already lent him a hundred pounds—by spying upon me? What ought I to do?"

VI.

I gave her a letter of introduction to an eminent solicitor, who speedily put a stop to the machinations of the spy, and then Miss Ogilvie Westerne, who

called upon me in a carriage and pair, attended by
obsequious flunkeys, informed me that she had resolved upon taking a house and sending for her
Scotch servants. A few days afterwards a house
agent wrote to me, as is usual, inquiring if Miss
Westerne was a responsible person. I replied, and
said what I knew and thought, but referred the appli-
cant to the lady's agents. Then I thought my wife
might call upon her ladyship, and she did. Further,
my wife took compassion upon her splendid loneliness,
and accepted a seat in her box at a fashionable West
End theatre.

VII.

The partner of my joys and sorrows, unfavourably
impressed with the lady's manners, said she must
decline to be seen in her company again, and while
she was detailing to me the eccentricities of Miss
Westerne, which she disliked, I received a letter
from my Edinburgh correspondent. He had been
misinformed as to the lady's antecedents. She was
not the woman he had taken her for. There were
strange rumours concerning her. She was wanted in
many quarters. He begged to withdraw his recommendation of her. Here was a *contretemps*. I saw
my lady the next day, laid this letter before her, and
asked for an explanation.

"Come with me, my dear sir," she said; "come

at once; my carriage is at the door. I will explain; but I beg of you to come to my house."

I went, to discover the perfidy of man in all its hideous colours. She showed me a packet of love letters from the North; showed me an offer of marriage from my epistolary friend.

IN THE PARK.

"I have refused him only this week, as you see, and he has sworn to be revenged, and this is his method. What do you think of a man who can be so base?"

"All that a man should think," I said; "your explanation is satisfactory."

VIII.

I wrote to my Edinburgh friend. He sent me an advertisement in which the lady was "wanted" indeed. Other circumstances excited my suspicions. I wrote to madame, requesting her to give me references

to her agents and solicitors, and until I had received
them begged her not to call upon me any more. She
replied in a dignified note, saying that she would
not trespass further upon my courtesy; some day I
should know her better, and when we met in Society
on that future day, I would, no doubt, apologise for
suspecting her. Then came letters from tradespeople
to whom she had mentioned me as a reference. I
wrote and requested Miss Westerne not to use my
name on pain of legal proceedings. She retorted
scornfully, and desisted, and presently came to live in
my neighbourhood with her maids and housekeepers,
her secretary and footmen, with her horses and
carriages and dogs. I did myself the honour of
cutting her dead, and cautioning everybody against
her. But she was so handsome, she looked so happy,
she drove such splendid cattle, she spoke Italian so
fluently, and became so popular with tradespeople and
local visitors, that I began to think I had made a
mistake, though I was contented to walk in the
shadow of my neighbour's magnificence.

IX.

Within three months the splendid bubble burst.
Miss Westerne's housekeeper, a fashionably-dressed
lady, was brought before the magistrates for swindling.
Her mistress succeeded in eluding the police. She

had been buying everything everywhere and selling her purchases again, and otherwise "spoiling the Egyptians" of the West End of pictures, jewellery, silks, satins, cabinets, and goods of the costliest kind. As fast as they were delivered at the front door, the treasures disappeared at the back. The housekeeper was remanded. Finally she was released on the bail of a gentleman who came forward and said he had lent her mistress a thousand pounds. She was not Miss Westerne at all, but a married woman. The police believed she had sailed for America, whither she had shipped large quantities of luggage. Soon afterwards I read an account in a foreign journal of a beautiful lady, whose charities and enterprises, literary, journalistic, and theatrical, had won the admiration of a colonial province. They called her "my lady," and she was about to marry a millionaire. I wonder if she is the fair horsewoman of my Scotch friend's short romantic dream. I bear her no animosity. If you should ever meet her, you will know her by her black eyes, her arched and pencilled brows, her white teeth, her tall, graceful figure, her pretty foot, and a slight Scotch accent that gives a siren-like music to her voice, which proved irresistible to many a wary Londoner during the merry days of a brilliant season.

X.

"A very good story," said Fox, "proving once more, to use a very hackneyed phrase, that 'truth is stranger than fiction.'"

"Of course truth *is* stranger than fiction," I said. "but in novels truth often seems more unreal than invention. The most astute of critics will now and then question the truthful incidents in a novel to praise for their reality passages which belong to the realms of pure imagination."

"No doubt," answers Fox; "and the annals of Scotland Yard are more tragic and romantic than all the novels that ever were written."

"More tragic, perhaps, but not more romantic, Fox; more tragic and more romantic than most of the novels that are based on criminal trials; but not so romantic as the great masterpieces of fiction."

"If I say 'offer material for fiction that no other repository of the world's tragedies, secret and public, can,' may I be allowed my opinion?" asked Fox, with his customary snap.

"By all means; this is a free country."

"Too free," was Fox's closing remark, "too free, the London streets at night, to wit; they could hardly be worse if all the foreign Governments selected the most abandoned specimens of their subjects to fling them into our midst, without question, registration, or record: London receives day by day the outcasts of France, Germany, Russia, and Italy to prey upon our industrial population and demoralise our streets."

"What is the remedy, Fox?"

"A registration of foreigners, and a return to their own countries of paupers and thieves. Put that into your next packet of cigarette papers."

XXIV.

LOST IN LONDON.

Burlesque and Art—Leslie and the Master—A Subject for a Novel—Drama in Real Life—An Incident of Victoria Station—Men and Women who Disappear—"Save me!"

I.

"WHAT do you think of the Gaiety fuss?" Fox asked, sitting with me at his Piccadilly Club, overlooking the street, while the autumn wind was chasing the leaves under the window whence we were watching the afternoon crowd on its usual afternoon parade.

"The Leslie burlesque of Irving?" I asked.

"Yes," Fox replied, handing me the cigarette-case

which a grateful royal client had presented to him at Homburg.

"I think Irving was right and Leslie wrong; and I am not sorry that the tragedian invoked authority in the cause of art and decency."

"Did you see the dance?"

"No," I replied, "but I admire Leslie's ability; he is a clever comedian, who might hold a distinguished place, if the opportunity offered, in the highest path of comedy."

"So might Nellie Farren," remarked Fox, "if she had not descended to burlesque; but there must be the opportunity."

"I knew Leslie some years ago in America, and said to him in person very much what I am saying to you; and I cannot understand how a man of his character and capacity could consent to dress himself up in short ballet-skirts to travesty the foremost man in his profession. Even the ablest and best of men have intellectual aberrations, and one must excuse Leslie on this ground."

"I rather like burlesque," Fox replied; "life itself is gloomy enough, without asking us to tax our feelings over mimic sorrows."

"That is a commonplace view," I said. "If it were worth anything it would simply put a broad insane grin upon art and make the world ridiculous. If life would be tolerable but for its pleasures as they now exist, what would it be if art were inspired by your cheap bit of tinselly philosophy?"

"Oh, if you take it in that way," said Fox, "let us change the subject."

"For what?"

"One you will like," he said, smiling; and as he said so the servants began to draw down the blinds, for the sun had set and the Piccadilly pedestrians had become shadowy.

II.

"I have accepted a rather curious commission."

"Professional?" I asked.

"Yes," he said, "and I am off to a little town in Germany to-night."

"Bank robbery?" I asked.

"No," he replied, "a criminal case; influence brought to bear upon me to take it up; have consented. Do you want a subject for a novel? Here is one."

Beckoning me into a quiet corner of the club, Fox, laying aside his cigarette, and composing himself into a calm attitude, said:—

"One misty day in July, a few months back, a pretty girl, well connected, left her home at Norwood to visit a sick friend at Bayswater. Her lover, to whom she was engaged, saw her off by the local train. She was to return at six, her father and mother dining at that hour. It was summer and she was lightly clad, but it looked like rain, and she carried an umbrella. 'I shall get a 'bus at Victoria,' she said. 'But if it rains take a cab,' responded her lover. Not a very romantic conversation you perceive: but they were to have been married within ten days of this little prosaic incident. Six o'clock came, and she did not return home—six, seven, eight; then her family grew anxious. The lover was sent for. They met every train until eleven; then he went off to London to the house where she was to have seen her sick friend; and in the lover's absence the father met every train until the last, and then he also started for London. The lover had already discovered that she had not been seen at Bayswater; the father obtained similar information; he called on other friends who might, perhaps, have received a visit from his daughter. No trace or sign of her anywhere. He and his prospective son-in-law then communicated with the police and made a tour of the hospitals; perhaps she had met with an accident and had been carried to one of these establishments insensible. All night long did the anxious couple traverse the great city from hospital to hospital, police-station to police-station; no result. The police made various suggestions as to her life and habits. Was it possible she had formed any attachment they did not know of? Utterly impossible. Was she very pretty? might she have been entrapped for some wrong purpose? She was pretty, very modestly dressed, her manner dignified, her love of home a passion, and her engagement to be married a satisfaction to all concerned. The police hinted that there had been cases of girls being lured away. The lover could not help remembering with a pang that Victoria was not the safest of stations for a young girl to be about alone; and the father upbraided himself for not having accompanied her. The police admitted that Victoria was a station in and around which bad characters assembled; and also spoke of wicked neighbourhoods close by. After giving every possible information to the police, father and prospective son-in-law went to Norwood father to his desolate home, prospective son-in-law to his lonely lodging. The next day the search went on; the next and the next; weeks passed, months—two; next week it will be three months. No clue not a vestige of a trace of

SHE WAS MODESTLY DRESSED.

the girl. Her mother has for days been at the verge of death or madness with grief; the father has done nothing but wander hither and thither, going to see everybody that is found dead under mysterious circumstances; the lover, in various disguises, getting inside every suspicious house about Victoria and between Victoria and Bayswater. No result."

III.

"I seem to have heard something like this story before," I remarked.

"If you were the head of the detective force at Scotland Yard you would hear similar stories continually. But many persons go away of their own accord, have arranged their mysterious disappearances beforehand. Some rather encourage the idea of murder to cover their retreat; men run away from their creditors; some from their wives; some elope with nice girls or equally attractive widows. There is a case in the papers just now, you know, where a Congregational minister at Walsall was supposed to have been murdered—a very ridiculous supposition in his case, he had done nothing worth a pin to be even threatened politically—and he is now engaged in the questionable delights of an illicit honeymoon. But the case of this girl I fear will develop tragically: she has been spirited away from England, after possibly enduring miseries beyond description on this side of the Channel."

IV.

"How do you know?" I asked.

"Two days ago," continued Fox, "a person high in authority came to me and told me the story I have related to you: then asked me to find the girl, and bring somebody to justice. He placed in my hands this card, which reached Norwood, addressed to the father, two days ago: '*Caselle, Germany: Save me—your lost child, Alice.*' And I am going to try and do it; so for the present, good-bye."

"With this romance in your thoughts, and that heart-breaking message in your pocket, you could yet talk of the Gaiety and——"

"The seriousness of life and its gloom and trouble," said Fox, interrupting me. "My dear friend, the stories of the London streets outstrip the imagination and invention of both dramatists and story-tellers. I have a theory about Alice. When I have tested it I will tell you what it is, and the result of my trip to Germany. The father started off by the very next train on receiving the message."

"Well?"

"That's all at present; must go now."

"Very sorry," I said, "you have excited my interest deeply."

"If this were a magazine story I dare say I might get you a proof of the finish and tell you how it ends. But this story is in progress and Fate is the prompter. *Au revoir!*"

XXV.

FOUND IN GERMANY.

Fox continues his Exciting Story—Worse than Death—A New Anaesthetic—Mother and Father—A Strange Feature of the Case—The Fiend who spoke French with a Foreign Accent.

I.

"YES, I have found her," said Fox, "but not him. Her father, as I told you, started ahead of me to the little German town. I question, though, if he knows the whole of her sad, sad story. He found her in the care of a religious society; she was utterly unlike her former self—weak, pale, emotional, and, I should say, more or less on the verge of brain fever. It is one of the most remarkable and terrible true stories of the London streets that has come within my knowledge."

"And that is very considerable and comprehensive, eh?"

"Yes, if I related my reminiscences I think I should startle the public. They would, however, have the consolation of not believing one-half of them."

"Oh, I don't know that. The romances of the newspapers eclipse all the inventions of the novelists. But here is your favourite brand," I said, indicating a flagon of old whisky, for it was late at night when Fox arrived, and there is no better night-cap than the mountain dew. I wish, at the same time, Fox had called during the day, for, though he left me comparatively early and I was very tired, the remembrance of his story kept me awake until daylight.

II.

"I don't want to make a romance out of it," said Fox. "You can elaborate it if you like; I dare say you will one of these days. If you do, I have one favour to ask: don't put it into three volumes; let it be crisp and short—price one shilling."

"In the meantime," I replied, "you shall tell it me for a bundle of 'Cigarette Papers.'"

"A gruesome one," he said, "I fear. But these are the plain, unvarnished facts. It appears that on that misty afternoon when the young lady arrived at Victoria Station, it was raining. She passed under the archway to the front for the purpose of taking an omnibus to Bayswater. Under the archway a man spoke to her with a curious accent, which she afterwards recalled as being something like French spoken by a Russian. The girl was highly educated, and clever as a linguist. She turned round, to find at her elbow a strange man. She did not speak, but hurried on to the omnibus. Unfortunately it was full. She put up her umbrella, and went forward a few yards to call a four-wheeler. Suddenly she heard the same voice that had accosted her under the archway by her side; an umbrella was suddenly thrust above her own, and a handkerchief pressed over her nostrils and mouth. She remembers nothing more until—how long afterwards she does not know—she found herself in what appeared to be a foreign house, attended by several women, who took it in turns to watch her—one of them an old hag who laughed at her sufferings. Needless to say, she was subjected to the worst kind of ill-treatment by the man who had succeeded in carrying her off. After some weeks of awful experiences in an immoral house abroad, the poor creature was permitted to make her escape; her gaolers fearing, no doubt, that they might have her death to account for if they detained her any longer. In a more or less delirious condition she wandered about the foreign town, and was finally taken by a priest to the house of a religious order, from whence she wrote the few words on the card I mentioned : '*Save me—your lost child, Alice.*'"

III.

" And the lover ? " I asked.

" Wild with grief."

" Does he know the story ? "

" I myself have told it him. It was best he should know it."

" Where is he ? "

" In Germany ; but they will not let him see her. He has sent affectionate messages to her ; is willing still to carry out his engagement, which she utterly and emphatically declines."

" It must have been a very powerful anæsthetic to have so promptly overcome the girl."

" Yes," said Fox. " The medical expert explained to the young lady's sorrowing friends that chloroform would not take effect in the open air, but that the anæsthetic used was no doubt one which has been adopted of late in Paris—very powerful and very prompt in its effects."

IV.

" And the mother," I asked, " what of her ? "

" Prostrated at home, in the hands of doctors and nurses. There are hopes of her recovery, but only a mother, I suppose, can imagine her grief. The father, on the other hand, is as strong and firm as a rock, without a sigh or a tear; a face capable, I should say, of expressing the kindliest emotions, and a man of very sympathetic nature; but to-day as rigid and as determined as an executioner. He is going to find that man who spoke to his daughter under the archway at Victoria; he is going to have by the throat the ruffian who no doubt put her into the very cab which she herself had hailed. It is hardly a question of theory. One can quite imagine it: the assailant accosting the cabman, and speaking of his daughter or his wife taken suddenly ill; possibly the cabman assisting him to lift her into his vehicle, and finally driving away, and helping the abductor to carry her into the house where she was evidently detained for some days. I grant you it is a very strange feature of the case, getting the girl

"THAT DEMON OF THE ARCHWAY WHO SPOKE FRENCH WITH A RUSSIAN ACCENT."

across the Channel ; but, after all, this would be easy in the case of a rich man, and more particularly a foreigner dealing with an invalid. There are invalid road carriages ; there are invalid railway carriages ; and, fortified with assistance, it would not be seriously difficult to get the poor girl away."

V.

"No, I grant you that," I said, "for I remember a case in America where a lady of position was attacked by two designing ruffians and conveyed by train to a den in New York, whence she was only rescued to eventually die of a broken heart. They represented that she was a lunatic, and they were her keepers. Being accosted at one place a little suspiciously, they produced their bogus warrant of official capture, and received, on the railway and at New York, assistance to get the poor mad creature into their power. But what of your foreign ruffian who spoke French with a Russian accent ?"

"Ah!" said Fox, "what indeed! At the moment not a trace of him ; at the moment very little trace in regard to the house where the girl was detained in London, and hardly any even in the city where she was found. I went through every hole and corner of the German town ; passed through every immoral house, found my way into the strangest and most wicked places ; always accompanied by the girl's father, rigid, strong, unrelenting. I have, however, induced him to go home to-day to comfort his wife, for the purpose of giving me a few days to hunt alone. I have an idea—it is shadowy at present—but I think I see looming up in the midst of it the form and features of that demon of the archway who spoke French with a Russian accent."

XXVI.

THE END OF THE DRAMA.

Cui Bono?—Questions of the Day and the Story of Victoria Station—Fox and Monsieur X——They discuss the French and English Systems, and Fox makes a Discovery—The Wretch meets his Master—Truth and Fiction—Finis.

I.

MET Fox a few days after our somewhat melodramatic chat about the startling abduction of the young lady from Victoria Station. I was walking home pondering the question of *Cui Bono?* which seems to be the great question of the day about everything, when I found Fox suddenly by my side.

"A fine night," he said, touching me on the shoulder.

"Is that your professional touch?" I asked.

"No," he replied, "nor my professional salutation."

"Glad to see you, Fox."

"Same to you," said Fox, cheerfully. "You were thinking?" said Fox, when we resumed our walk.

"Yes," I said, "'Is marriage a failure?' 'Is life worth living?' 'Does cold tub do more harm than good?' 'Is Oxford a fraud?' 'What's the good of going to receptions?'"

"The interrogations of the press," said Fox; "they remind me of those old advertising questions, 'Do you bruise your oats?' 'Who's Griffiths?' The general answer might be in vulgar parlance, 'What's the odds so long as you're happy?'"

"Ben Webster suggested a reply to 'Who's Griffiths,' you remember? The placarded question was on the walls at the time of the first production of *The Dead Heart*, and Webster wanted to put underneath the poster 'Watts Phillips.'"

"Ah," said Fox, "I don't see the application."

"Watts Phillips was the author of *The Dead Heart*," I said.

"Oh, was he!" said Fox, who, however much he knows of life in general, is not as well up in theatrical history as he might be.

II.

"'Who's Griffiths?' 'Watts Phillips!' don't quite see it; too subtle for the likes of I," said Fox, laughing; and then with his own particular snap of the thin lips, adding, "but I found him."

"You did!" I exclaimed, for I had been thinking all the time of the Frenchman who spoke with a Russian accent, and he knew it.

What a habit we all have of talking of everything else but the one subject we mean to talk about, until one or other of the parties to the conversation conceives that the time for the main subject has arrived.

"A pale, cadaverous, morbid sensualist, a Russian who had lived in France for twenty years; rich, a mesmerist, hypnotist, theosophist, and the rest," said Fox, hurrying on with his story. "I left the father of the girl at home, as I told you; went to Paris, saw my friend Monsieur X——, the greatest of detective experts of our time—keen, suave, with eyes that look right into your very soul. 'They all make the mistake of too much repetition,' said Monsieur X——: 'the fascination of success is a criminal basilisk; were it not so how much more difficult our work would be, Monsieur Fox,' he remarked, thoughtfully twirling his moustache. 'That is so, no doubt; and yet how often has a certain fiend in London repeated his murderous offence,' I replied. 'It is true,' said the famous French detective; 'but you have too much freedom in England.'

III.

"'Too much freedom, and yet we are a monarchy and you are a republic,' I replied," continued Fox.

"'But you extend your freedom to thieves and murderers; we draw the line at crime. And, moreover, you give your police authority, but do not allow them to use it. You give them a baton, but they must keep it in their pockets. You say, "Find out the thief, but you must not go into a house after him without a warrant;" while you get the warrant your thief has gone away. Too much liberty for criminals—that is the difficulty of the detective service in London. I would find that Jack for you if you gave me full authority, but not as it is with you at present; you give your Jack too much of a start in the race.'
'I have no doubt you are right, Monsieur,' I said. 'How would it have been,' he continued, 'with this Monsieur Straveletzky if I had had to wait for the warrant? There is an abduction. She is a young lady of good family. He will have nothing to do with them if they are not of good family. Unhappily she is of great spirit. She throws herself out of a tall high storey in the Rue de Bach—it is her death. I happen to be passing at the moment. I go into the house. I come upon the confederate of the Russian hypnotist sensualist. I take him by the throat. "Confess," I say; "where is he? You will not tell? Come, then." I hand him over to my officers. The next day he tells all; and it may be he knows of this young lady in the German town. There are letters in the Russian's desk from C―― in Germany. Is

that your town?' 'The same,' I said. 'Come, we will interrogate him.'

IV.

"It was only a short drive. The prison doors flew open, as doors flew in the Arabian story, at the magic

word. In a few minutes we were in the governor's room, and a pale, cunning, creepy-looking wretch was brought in by a warder. 'You remember the month of July last year, the tenth?' 'No,' said the prisoner. 'You were at Victoria Station, in London?' 'No,' was the reply; but at the same time the prisoner looked round uneasily, as if he thought there was some one at his elbow. 'Your assistant has confessed.'

'He was not with me,' said the prisoner quickly, and with a little triumphant chuckle. 'But he knows all about it, and the house at C——, where you stayed with her.' 'You have hypnotised me!' exclaimed the prisoner. 'You have the art of the seers. It is not an equal duel. I am only the amateur. You are the Unknowable. I will be your ally. The Kabala shall give us all! Hush!' 'Mad!' said Monsieur X——; 'this is no simulation.' The prisoner raised his right hand, made signs, and concluded with passes in the air. 'I bow before the master—the unknown essence. What would you——?' 'You remember July of last year?' 'Yes,' said the prisoner, smiling a ghastly smile of knowledge, as if he would say, 'We both now remember it.' 'The tenth of the month?' 'Yes, Kabala,' he said; 'yes, Theages, it was I!' And so on. I don't want to make a long story of it. For a time it was difficult to know whether he was not saying 'Yes' and 'No' at random; but his confederate gave us all the missing links. He had met the wretch with his victim at Calais, and had travelled with them in the character of a physician to the German town. I spare you the details; you can guess them. The methodical maniac had used the anæsthetic, and, furthermore, was shown to possess a certain mesmeric power. But here are your chambers, and it is time to say Good night or Good morning."

"One word more," I said; "about the father?"

"He is more resigned to his fate now. The doctors have warned him that upon him depends the life of his wife. He is not to leave her; she may die if he does—this he understands. I saw him yesterday, and told him the man was safe for a life's imprisonment, even if he escapes the guillotine. He wants to see the fiend. My advice is against it; but if he persists, by-and-bye I shall go to Paris with him, and he can inspect the wild beast whom Monsieur X—— has caged. And when you have influence enough to get the London police some of the special powers enjoyed by their French confrères, Scotland Yard may be trusted to bring to light the demon of Whitechapel. Good night!"

It was morning. A greyish-red light was embellishing the north-western suburb. Policemen in couples conversed lazily at the corners of streets. Night-cabs were rumbling homewards. The morning light had almost put out my hall gas. I drew my blinds against both gas and sunshine, and tried not to think of that poor victim away in the kindly security of the sisters of the distant religious house, and the broken-hearted father and mother at the other side of London. Is life worth living indeed? Ask them!

FINIS.

www.ingramcontent.com/pod-product-compliance
Lightning Source LLC
Chambersburg PA
CBHW022020240426
43667CB00042B/1011